I'm encouraged by reading this and Dr. Freeman has reminded me that God has planned an incredible journey for each of us. This book will help many others as we travel along whatever journey God has ordained for our lives.....And if we remain steadfast as he has, we will certainly be rewarded. Something BIG is about to happen to this great husband and father.

Melissa Fulmore-Hardwick

Nearly twenty years ago, watching Paul and Vivian exchange vows, I had no idea the faith journey that was ahead. This book shows the deep abiding passion and faith of a Godly man who is sent into a Job-like situation and still retains his integrity. Paul Freeman teaches us how to stand when we don't understand what God is doing! A Must Read for Every Believer!

Pastor Clifford Johnson,
Zion Hope Baptist Church

Ambushed:
An Uplifting Story by a Determined Man

Dr. Paul L. Freeman, Jr.

WESTBOW
PRESS®
A DIVISION OF THOMAS NELSON
& ZONDERVAN

Scripture taken from the New King James Version. Copyright © 1979, 1980,
1982 by Thomas Nelson, Inc. Used by permission. All rights reserved.

Scripture taken from the King James Version of the Bible.

Scripture taken from the Holy Bible, NEW INTERNATIONAL VERSION®.
Copyright © 1973, 1978, 1984 by Biblica, Inc. All rights reserved worldwide.
Used by permission. NEW INTERNATIONAL VERSION® and NIV® are
registered trademarks of Biblica, Inc. Use of either trademark for the offering
of goods or services requires the prior written consent of Biblica US, Inc.

WestBow Press books may be ordered through booksellers or by contacting:

WestBow Press
A Division of Thomas Nelson & Zondervan
1663 Liberty Drive
Bloomington, IN 47403
www.westbowpress.com
1 (866) 928-1240

Because of the dynamic nature of the Internet, any web addresses or
links contained in this book may have changed since publication and
may no longer be valid. The views expressed in this work are solely those
of the author and do not necessarily reflect the views of the publisher,
and the publisher hereby disclaims any responsibility for them.

Any people depicted in stock imagery provided by Thinkstock are models,
and such images are being used for illustrative purposes only.
Certain stock imagery © Thinkstock.

ISBN: 978-1-5127-0592-8 (sc)
ISBN: 978-1-5127-0593-5 (e)

Library of Congress Control Number: 2015912201

Print information available on the last page.

WestBow Press rev. date: 08/04/2015

Acknowledgements

First, and foremost, thanks to God, my source and strength, for inspiring me to write this book based on my personal situation and the challenges I have encounter from the day Vivian, my wife, was diagnosed with Multiple Sclerosis (MS) to the present. My only prayer is that at least one person will be encouraged as a result of reading this book; if one person is encouraged, then this book has not been in vain.

Let me shout a big "THANK YOU" to all of you who have provided support to my family through your many acts of kindness which include your prayers, meals, financial assistance, visits to the nursing home, watching the girls (Ariana, Ashlyn & Aniyah), and your words of encouragement.

Thank you, God, for a Mom who has taught me to be the responsible man I am today.

Thank you, God, for my Pastor, Dr. Eugene Diamond and my church family - Abyssinia Missionary Baptist Church. Thank you, God, for my extended family and my true friends you have blessed me with.

In Memory of the Late Bishop Tom E. Diamond, a great and wonderful man who is truly missed by so many people because of the impact he had on their lives. He was a man who took me under his wings and treated me as his own son. He was the man whom I saw as "Dad".

Special Thanks to Tosha, my best friend, for the last twenty-five plus years. Words could never express my sincere appreciation for all the sacrifices and support you have rendered.

Special Thanks to my agent, Joy Bradley-Walker, who has constantly reminded me God would hold me accountable if I did not finish at least one book.

Dedication

This book is dedicated to
Ariana Alexis, Ashlyn Alexandria, & Aniyah Alexia,
my three beautiful daughters.
My Prayer is that you will always rely on the
power of God to provide you the strength and
tenacity to deal with the unexpected.
LOVE ALWAYS,

DADDY

Foreword

My father, the late Bishop Tom E. Diamond, always said that Dr. Paul Freeman was one of the most organized persons he had ever met. Paul was meticulous for planning out every aspect of his day, his week, his month, his year and his life. From dating Vivian, to completing college, to getting married and having two children, Paul had his life completely planned out. That was until he came crashing into my father's office in an emotional mess because his perfectly planned life had just been unexpectedly interrupted. With he and Vivian now well focused on their careers and raising their two beautiful girls, they were completely not ready for what the doctor informed them. Vivian Was Pregnant!

For years my father jokingly told of Paul's frantic conversation that day in his office saying, "this can't be," "we were finished having children," (and my father's favorite line from Paul) "This is not how I planned it to be." My father reminded Paul, and the rest of us, that God doesn't always follow our plans because sometimes God has other plans for our lives. And for Paul and Vivian, God knew their lives would not be complete without little Ms. Aniyah.

In the years that followed, Paul learned that God's plan was drastically different from his. It's from this perspective that Paul writes this book, simply entitled, <u>Ambushed</u>.

In this latest work of his, Dr. Paul Lance Freeman allows his readers to audit the classes of his life and learn lessons that Life has so poignantly presented. While there are some classes on the schedule that seem impossible to pass, Dr. Freeman transparently demonstrates to his readers how one's walk with God allows you to successfully matriculate through Life's most difficult courses. Although, as readers, we are simply auditing these Life courses with Dr. Freeman, we are allowed to take our own Spiritual Evaluation Test at the end. Also as a bonus Dr. Freeman has included a 40 day devotional which may aid in improving one's test score.

As pastor of the Abyssinia Missionary Baptist Church, where Dr. Freeman serves as Sunday School Superintendent, I have watched him shoulder the load of caregiving husband, faithful father, professor, and business man all while working faithfully in the church. As Superintendent, Dr. Freeman has written multiple curriculums for Sunday School, Children's Church, and Leadership Trainings.

Dr. Paul Freeman has an earned Ph.D. in Business Management from Nova University and currently serves as a Professor of Organizational Development for the University of Phoenix. It's from his academic perspective that Dr. Freeman writes about his life experiences. However, he doesn't present them from the perspective of a teacher, but from that of a student. A student enrolled in some of Life's most difficult courses.

Dr. Freeman's fun-loving personality can be seen throughout the book. And his sense of humor rescues you from your tears in some of the difficult chapters of his life. As a church family, we continue to pray for Vivian knowing that there is nothing too hard for God. And we continue to encourage and cheer on Paul and the girls as they continue to move successfully into the new chapters of their lives.

Dr. Freeman unselfishly reveals his soul and family in
<u>Ambushed</u>.
Definitely a must read.
Dr. Eugene W. Diamond
Senior Pastor – Abyssinia Missionary Baptist Church
Jacksonville, Florida

Contents

Preface

Sometimes it appears there is no end in sight from my two full time jobs; one being my employment from 8:00 a.m. to 5:00 p.m., the other being all of the job duties and responsibilities associated with being a husband and father caring for a spouse with a debilitating disease while raising three daughters. Prevailing laboriously and with a relentless spirit, now I realize nobody has a life without struggles. Invited or uninvited, sickness has a way of delaying or altering dreams just as five o'clock traffic can cause one to miss an important appointment.

I am a family man and husband, married to Vivian, a woman who was once full of life, a virtuous woman who has been battling with MS for thirteen years. Many days I find myself gazing over her body attempting to imagine how it feels to have a body with limbs that no longer function. The arms are incapable of swinging or hugging. Her legs that can't walk. Her eyes provide double vision. Her nose picks up aromas while salivary glands work as designed and, yet, her mouth has been hindered from chewing.

I am the father of three beautiful daughters who have already proven their ability to accept their mom's illness while demonstrating an appreciation for life and low tolerance for children who disrespect their mother. Some view having a mother as nothing special, but these three young ladies would give anything just to have a mother-daughter day.

In reading this book, I hope you will be encouraged regardless of your present situation. Please know that I did not write this book because I consider myself a perfect example of God's vessel. In fact, I'm very far from it. I wrote this book because becoming a vessel God can use has been and continues to be a far more painful journey than one can ever imagine. I hope to minister to you from the pain I have felt for the past thirteen years.

As I share my story with transparency, I only ask that you do not pass judgment on me, but respect me for being truthful because I realize there are some things contained within the pages of this book that you may disagree with or even feel are cruel thoughts. But, know this experience has caused me to think of the unthinkable. Additionally, it has generated feelings I didn't know I was capable of birthing.

Simply put, the goal of this book is to share the many lessons I have learned and continue to learn each day about coping with the unexpected. Furthermore, may you receive comfort in your present situation.

Blessed be God, even the Father of our Lord Jesus Christ, the Father of mercies, and the God of all comfort; Who comforteth us in all our tribulation, that we may be able to comfort them which are in any trouble, by the comfort wherewith we ourselves are comforted of God.
II Corinthians 1: 3, 4.

Words of the Day

Cope *verb*
1. to struggle or deal, especially on fairly even terms or with some degree of success (usually followed by with) 2. to face and deal with responsibilities, problems, or difficulties, especially successfully or in a calm or adequate manner
cope. (n.d.). *Dictionary.com Unabridged*. Retrieved June 19, 2015, from Dictionary.com website: http://dictionary.reference.com/browse/cope

Un-ex-pect-ed *adjective*
1. not expected; unforeseen; surprising
unexpected. (n.d.). *Dictionary.com Unabridged*. Retrieved June 16, 2015, from Dictionary.com website: http://dictionary.reference.com/browse/unexpected

Two simple words that have changed my life.

CHAPTER ONE

Paul & Vivian

From the Latin root name Paul.

Small

- Expression -

Loves to keep everyone laughing

- Personality -

Has a lot of vision and inspiration

- Natural -

Capable of learning great things

- Emotional -

Someone who is full of contentment

Dr. Paul L. Freeman, Jr.

- Character -

Gives a shoulder to lean on and shares himself

- Physical -

Serves Everyone

- Mental -

A most enlightened person

- Motivation -

A very dedicated person

**1991 P.M.A. Names & Faces Vernal, Ut.
USA (D & B) Computer Concepts**

From the Latin root name Vivian.

Full of Life

- Expression -

Aboveboard in all things

- Personality -

Someone who is a likeable person

- Natural -

Takes time for gifted people

- Emotional -

She is virtuous

- Character -

Her integrity and name are priceless to her

- Physical -

Has appealing appearances

- Mental -

Has a good day when she learns something new

Dr. Paul L. Freeman, Jr.

- *Motivation* -

Holds steadfast to her course [1]

---

[1] 1991 P.M.A. Names & Faces Vernal, Ut. USA (D & B) Computer Concepts

It was the summer of 1986 and I had just graduated from high school and was in the process of preparing to embark upon my freshman year of college at the University of North Florida. Vivian, in contrast, was preparing to enter the 11th grade at William M. Raines High School. August 13, 1986 was the official date we became a couple, and on October 31, 1992 I proposed and we became engaged. We courted for a total of seven years prior to marriage. We became the model couple at church because of the Christian standards we maintained during our courtship. It was common knowledge that we both were virgins and remained virgins until we married on June 26, 1993. We were both recent college graduates each working a full-time job, which enabled us to purchase our home within the first year of our marriage. So, from my perspective we had done everything correctly and were guaranteed to have a successful marriage and family. Yes, I knew we would deal with some of the typical challenges that marriages experience within the first five years – communication issues, learning and coping with each other's imperfections, dealing with differences that seem nonessential when dating, but become center stage after marriage, and learning how to balance work and family once kids came into the picture.

After all, I was the Sunday school teacher for married couples; therefore, our marriage would be an excellent example for other couples in the church. As a Sunday school teacher, I was constantly encouraging and motivating couples while aiming to be a Godly spouse and father. In summary, as a couple, we were traveling a road that had a few speed bumps; but, for the most part, it was a good road, one with no bend in the foreseeable future. Yes, we were young and enjoying life. We lived in a middle-class neighborhood, with everything except the white picket fence. We were two working professionals with expectations of a limitless future, a future where we envisioned raising kids, traveling, pursuing entrepreneurship opportunities and reaching our elderly years together. As a happily married couple, I recall moments where "welcome to our world" became a phrase we constantly used because it was a world full of dreams and an optimistic outlook on life. It seemed as if our world was allowing us to become impregnated with dreams daily. For Vivian, there was the dream of establishing a five star beauty and spa salon. For me, there was a dream of traveling the world and offering professional development seminars for fortune 500 organizations. However, our dreams had to confront the harsh reality of being placed on hold due to being AMBUSHED by a terrible disease.

The rain has subsided, and it's Friday evening as I'm sitting in a restaurant alone and quietly, waiting for the waitress to bring my meal. While patiently waiting, I began to survey the guests assembled in the restaurant and noticed several couples within my view. There were two older couples to my right, probably in their early 60s, looking as if they have raised their kids and were enjoying retirement. Directly to my left were two young couples that appeared to be happily married and probably had no kids. To my immediate rear, there were two middle-aged couples with their kids. It was the scenery of the various couples that caused me to have a melancholy mood – the young couples caused me to reminisce of how things were when Vivian and I first met; the middle-aged couples caused my mind to be dominated by the thoughts of all the things Vivian and I would not be able to do as a family with our daughters; the older couples made me feel as if Vivian and I were being robbed of the opportunity to grow old together. I realized we would have no story of how we raised our daughters together. Now, to my surprise, I realized life had brought me to a bend in the road that I never expected, a bend that has become a journey but has not reached its final destination.

CHAPTER TWO

The Unexpected

Here's how it began. It all commenced on a cool breezy day in November 2001 when Vivian, my wife, started experiencing headaches with excruciating pain. The headaches were constant and there was no sign of relief from the pain. As a result, Vivian notified her primary physician, and he had her come to the office for a visit. At that time he conducted several standard tests hoping he could identify the root cause of Vivian's headaches. The standard tests revealed nothing out of the ordinary so he provided Vivian a referral to a neurologist.

In January 2002, Vivian went to see the first neurologist and he scheduled Vivian for an MRI in an effort to determine the cause of the headaches. His diagnosis was good news because he stated the headaches were due to sinus problems. She was relieved and immediately started taking the sinus medication prescribed to her by the neurologist. As time went on, she appeared to be doing better; but suddenly, the headaches resurfaced.

After repeating the same routine with her primary physician, Vivian went to see a second neurologist. He immediately scheduled Vivian for an MRI. The results revealed signs of Multiple Sclerosis (MS) so he conducted one additional test, the spinal tap. Based on the color of the spinal fluid, we knew this final test would end any speculation and provide us good or bad news. I was attempting to maintain a positive outlook and not draw any premature conclusion until we received the results of the spinal tap.

The appointed day and hour had finally arrived for the results to be revealed by the neurologist. As I looked the neurologist in the eyes and watched the words flow out of his mouth, he announced politely and calmly, "You have multiple sclerosis." Vivian was told she had a form of MS titled Chronic Progressive, which meant the disease would progressively get worse. I felt like I was caught in category 5 hurricane with no means of escape. It's amazing how your life can change in one day, from sunshine to a severe storm with winds in excess of 155 miles per hour.

Upon digesting the terrible news, Vivian started taking physical therapy as a strategy to maintain her mobility. However, the disease became more progressive on a daily basis and the proof was right before my very eyes as I read the letter addressed to the insurance company from the treating neurologist:

To Whom It May Concern: I am the treating neurologist caring for Mrs. Vivian Freeman. As you are aware, she carries a diagnosis of multiple sclerosis. Specifically, she has relapsing remitting multiple sclerosis, with secondary progression. As you are likely aware, she has had a very severe course and continues to gain additional disability, despite attempts at ameliorating her course. She has shown obvious and significant progression of disease on both Avonex as well as Copaxone. She was recently hospitalized for a course of IV Methylprednisolone for worsening vision and coordination. An MRI performed while in the hospital in June of 2004, compared with the January 2004 scan showed obvious progression of disease. We are undertaking placing her on Betaseron, and stabilizing her over a three to six month period. If she continues to show progression of disease, on Betaseron, we may opt to go with a more aggressive dual approach in terms of treatment. Mrs. Freeman is extremely debilitated. She is wheelchair bound, has virtually no strength in her legs, and severe incoordination in her upper extremities. She is in need of twenty-four hour care. As you may be aware, her husband is her sole support and works full time. They have three young children. I would strongly urge that Mrs. Freeman have assistance five half days, with regard to home health. She also needs a hoyer lift which actually fits the bed she has. Once graciously provided for however, it was inadequate with regard to use with her bed. Her husband and other care givers have to give her full assist to transfer her into and out of bed as a well from a wheel chair, to the bedside commode, or into the tub, et cetera.

Vivian went from a cane, to a walker, and then to a wheelchair in a matter of three months. All physical activities such as driving, bathing, and going to the bathroom quickly came to an end. Although she was coherent, scratching her nose and wiping tears from her eyes had become chores she could no longer perform. Swallowing became a chore and a close call to death due to food going down the wrong pipe, resulting in constant choking.

Today, Vivian has basically lost her mobility and has been declared disabled. The disease has changed her life, my life and the lives of our children.

CHAPTER THREE

The Road of Unbelief

During the winter semester of 2002, life enrolled me in my first course entitled "Unbelief 101" at Life on Earth University (LOEU). After an hour long consultation session with the Registrar Office, it was determined that I could not drop the course nor substitute another course in its place. Now that I have been in the course for quite some time, I have found it to be one of my most interesting and challenging courses at LOEU. Furthermore, this course has earned me the necessary continuing education hours required for learning how to cope with the unexpected.

Each day as I went to class the only thought that resonated in my mind was "could this really be happening to me?" I felt as if my finger was in an electrical socket while sitting in a bath tub of water. I was shocked. A part of me was in denial because I was only thirty three years old coupled with the fact that Vivian and I had only been married for eight years. No one could have ever told me I would be confronted with such a devastating situation. I was a Deacon and Sunday school teacher trying to live a pleasing and acceptable life to and for God. I had allowed myself to be deceived by the popular notion going around in churches today. And that is,

Christians have immunity from problems, pain or suffering. Now, I was being forced to face the reality that bad things really do happen to good people. I quickly learned MS did not care about my family nor me.

- MS didn't care about how much stress, pain, heartache, depression or any other emotion formulating in my body.
- MS didn't care that my three daughters would be without a mother in the traditional sense.
- MS didn't care that my life would be totally different as a husband and father.
- MS was not concerned about my credit score with Equifax or Transunion; nor was it concerned with all of the financial struggles it would generate in my life.

For days, I remember sitting on my bed and wishing this was a dream or movie on Lifetime Movie Network. Some days as I walked alone the bank of the river, I wondered if the unbelief would have been minimized had I seen the ambush coming. The thought never occurred to me that I, too, would be next in line to experience an episode of unbelief. I wanted to travel Faith Boulevard and hope that this would disappear through some magical act.

In addition, I recall days when the unbelief was so strong that all I wanted was to go back into the womb of my mother. I wanted to be an infant again or return to my childhood days. I just didn't want to bring myself to believe or accept the very truth that was right before my eyes. All I could think was I am too young for this and definitely did not sign up for this when I said "I Do" at the marriage ceremony on June 26, 1993. My marriage vows were forcing me to make a commitment to a very uncertain future based on an unpredictable disease. To be perfectly honest, I felt as if I was all alone and stuck in a bad situation which I had no control over.

For the past thirteen years I have been:

- Devastated, but not defeated
- Forsaken by a few friends, but supported by a faithful God
- Emotionally damaged, but not emotionally destroyed

The mental, emotional, and financial impact has been greater than anything I could have ever imagined, but now I understand that unbelief was a necessary chapter of life. However, it can't be the final chapter.

CHAPTER FOUR

Every Day Challenges

After completing my first course, *Unbelief 101*, I decided to take the summer semester off; at least that's what I thought. However, to my surprise I received a letter from LOEU informing me that the continuing education program was designed as a "non-stop" program and students were not allowed to take a break. Furthermore, the letter stated that I would automatically be enrolled in my next course and will include the syllabus as outlined below.

Challenge Course - 201
(Course Syllabus)

There is no one like you! Life's Challenge Course is a one of a kind experience and LOEU supports the opportunity for students to grow via real life challenges that surface in their lives and are beyond their control. The value students will receive by successfully accomplishing the Course will be life changing for the better and will give students an experience that will help them work through challenging situations. Students will be given opportunities to find and strengthen their faith while helping other Christians realize they can weather the storm. This *course will offer students an opportunity to view personal challenges combined with perceived limitations from a different perspective. However, please note that students do not reserve the right to opt out of any of the **Every Day Challenges** that will be presented.*

I must admit that I was not thrilled after reading the course syllabus. As a matter of fact, I was more discouraged and really did not think I could handle the course. I, nevertheless, came to the realization that the course was not optional but mandatory. Consequently, I printed off the syllabus and thought about how I would prepare myself for the journey of faith which was being thrust upon me.

The Challenges:

Every day I had to look at my wife knowing there was nothing I could do to reverse the disease. Medication, doctors, or therapy could not change her condition. Since the version of MS she has is considered chronic progressive, I had to watch her body transition to a debilitating state very quickly. For example, seeing food fly across the kitchen table as she attempted to feed herself was worse than the mess a two year old would make. No words can explain or describe the mental and emotional impact of watching your loved one move from a state of good health to needing you to do everything for them.

Richard Pryor, a renowned comedian, was diagnosed with the disease in 1986. Upon reading his story, my mind became saturated with thoughts of how long would the journey be for me. For example, by the early 1990s, he was confined to using a wheelchair as well as a motor powered scooter for the remainder of his life to get around when his MS began to take its toll on his body. I clearly remember my response the day I heard the evening news in 2005 announce that he had passed away, As I was sitting on the sofa, I said to myself, *"God, he had the disease for 19 years. I cannot imagine being in this situation for another sixteen years (since it was only the third year for me). God, I can't do this."*

My entire body, consequently, became numb just from the thought of the possibility of dealing with the situation for 19 years. In essence, one of the daily challenges continues to be dealing with all of the thoughts that go through my mind like the bright sunlight permeating through a room.

Every year the Greater Jacksonville Agricultural Fair is held from late October through mid November. It offers a variety of games, activities and rides for all ages. If you are a lover of roller coasters, then this is one event I would strongly recommend. Personally, I have never been a big fan of roller coasters…there are just too many loops and turns for me. But often times I find myself wishing I was on a roller coaster at the Jacksonville Agricultural Fair instead of this roller coaster ride of emotions, including fear, optimism, despair and hope. It's a ride that has created emotional turmoil in every area of my life. In some ways, I realize life will never be the same, but I must continue to find strategies for dealing with the emotional turmoil.

Although I consider the every day challenges to be disruptive moments, I'm learning to view them as divine appointments. As much as I don't want to deal with the daily challenges, I have discovered God selected me for this experience based on my Spiritual Resume. Furthermore, since God Himself is the Director of Human Resources, I can't be overlooked for the job based on insufficient qualifications. The challenges have taught me to look at Job as an example. Remember Job was a righteous man minding his own business; and yet, God gave Satan permission to test him, but with certain limitations. I find the story of Job so encouraging because it has taught me that God has total control and the final word. Also, the story demonstrates that we must change our perspective of the situation. Every unforeseen or disruptive moment will bring spiritual transformation and allow us to experience a side of God we have never encountered.

Strategies for Coping with Your Crisis:

Here are a few strategies I have learned from my experience. Please note I don't pretend to have mastered all of these points, but hopefully, you can benefit from my struggle.

1. **Denial vs. Divine Appointment.** First, it is important to remember that our refusal to acknowledge the situation doesn't make it disappear. While denial may be an initial reaction, it should never be the final reaction. Please don't misunderstand me. I can relate to ignoring or minimizing the seriousness of a situation while hoping that this approach will cause the situation to cease in its existence. But more importantly, we must learn that is okay to acknowledge the situation. I have found the best medicine for denial is TIME. My advice is view denial as one stage in the process of God moving you from where you are to where He will have you to be. Simply stated, denial is a process with a beginning, middle and end. We as humans must make sure we don't get stuck at the beginning or the middle. In regards to divine appointments, remember they are set by God and cannot be cancelled by man. Yes, the divine appointment may produce pain, but it is not pain without a prescription. God always provides us a

prescription with instructions. But, just like any other medicine, we must follow the instructions in order for the prescription to work as designed.

2. **Live in the Present** One common mistake I made is that I was constantly looking too far backward or too far forward, not realizing neither could help me. Somewhere in the process of dealing with the situation, I discovered I was existing but really not living. It was a feeling of being stuck between the past and the future and not knowing how to live in the present. Once I learned illness doesn't diminish humanity it enabled me to transition from living in the past or future to living in the moment. In essence, I began to live in the moment with patience, compassion and appreciation for life itself. Each day became a celebration for life because I took the advice of David in Psalm 118:24 when he stated, *"This is the day that the Lord has made and I shall rejoice and be glad in it."* I began to rejoice, not because the situation changed, but because each day was still a good day. See, a bad situation doesn't mean you have to have a bad day. For each day is a new day: a day of peace, grace, joy, and an appointed purpose. Remember, the situation doesn't change the fact that it's still the Lord's day. *More to come in Chapter 5 – Keep Reading!!*

3. **Know Your Enemy!** The more I learned about Vivian's disease, the more I was able to understand the changes I was observing. This enabled me to better empathize and become a more positive force and focus on my behavior. Sometimes out of frustration, I felt like my wife was the enemy, but the disease is the true enemy.

Remember, never attack your loved one; attack the enemy.

4. **Remember Who God Is.** Many times when we experience a bend in the road we lose perspective of the presence and power of God. As I travel this unexpected road, I am constantly reminded we serve an ever present God who has promised us that He will never leave nor forsake us. He is El-Shaddai, which means He is the All Sufficient and Almighty God. He is the God that is more than enough. The fact that God never sleeps is comforting in and of itself. I will admit that many days I have wished I could make a U-turn and get off this unexpected road I am traveling. However, I am reminded that God is always at work, even when He doesn't provide me a detailed agenda of His plan. There are days when I feel He has forgotten me because nothing seems to be going in my favor, but those are the days when God reminds me that He is a constant presence with me. To state it simply, we must always be reminded that as long as we are known by God, then we are never alone, isolated or forsaken.

> *Trouble may come into your day, but don't let trouble come into your heart.*
> **Tom Diamond**

CHAPTER FIVE

Sunday Mornings

Worship in the Storm - 301
(Course Syllabus)

This course helps you to understand the importance of individual worship. Attention will be given to how to maintain a heart of worship when you may be spiritually dehydrated. It is designed to show you how to worship even when hindrances are present in your life. Although this course is not designed to equip you to be a worship leader, it will help you understand that you must become an individual worshipper before you can become a corporate worshipper.

It's approximately 4:30 a.m. Sunday morning. It was too early for the sun to pierce through the clouds as I awaken to the loud buzzing sound of the alarm clock. Sunday mornings are many things to many people. For some it is a day of worship and fellowship, and a day of rest for others; but for me, it was a day of mixed emotions. While I looked forward to morning service, I was not overly thrilled with the necessary tasks required for Vivian and three kids in order to be at worship service by 7:15 a.m.

The first task was to get Vivian in the shower and cleaned-up, which required removing a soiled diaper, a diaper capable of containing urine, bowel movement or discharges of blood from her menstrual cycle, and in some cases, it was comprised of all three. It took God and his angels just to keep me from having an emotional and a mental breakdown. All I could do is whisper a silent pray and say "God, please give me the strength. For I am weak, but in you I am strong." Words can't express how difficult it is to witness your love one migrate from a position of good health (independent) to a state requiring total assistance (dependent).

Over time it became more and more challenging with dressing Vivian. For example, I would lift her to her feet from the wheelchair, and then my two oldest daughters, ages 7 and 5 at that time, would pull her pants up while I held her up. It truly took teamwork to get Vivian dressed.

After getting Vivian completely dressed, I would start breakfast in an effort to avoiding hearing growling stomachs during service. Once everyone was fed and the kitchen was cleaned, I would start dressing the kids. Since they were so young I had to dress them one at a time from the oldest to the youngest. I never dreamed of the day when I would be dressing three girls, combing and accessorizing hair.

After dressing all the ladies, it was time for me hasten to the shower and get dress because 7:15 a.m. was quickly approaching. Once I was dressed, everyone was loaded into the vehicle, which required me to become Mr. T, without all the jewelry and unique haircut, because I had to physically lift Vivian from the wheelchair into the vehicle followed by loading the wheelchair into the vehicle. Now, off we go to the house of worship, sometimes on time and other times a few minutes late, but we made it there. Once there, I had to unload the wheelchair and lift Vivian from the SUV to the wheelchair while the kids patiently waited on the sidewalk.

It was this experience that taught me we never know what people go through just to get to the place of worship, and we should be thankful if we are able to get to the house of worship without being confronted with Sunday morning challenges.

On many occasions, it was as if I was trying to put a bottle cap on a volcano in order to stop the challenges of Sunday morning from exploding in my life. However, I didn't have a Spiritual or Pentecostal plan designed for Sunday morning challenges. It was then that I realized Sunday morning was just like any other day, a day for coping with unexpected circumstances. It could be a day full of joy or full of pain. Some days I wished I had a private physician or anesthesiologist who could give me a shot or provide me a capsule to help me sleep through and alleviate the mental and emotional pain.

Sunday mornings became a constant reminder to me that into each life some rain must fall. Without the rain, we would never enjoy the sunshine. Please note: it's not that I couldn't cope with the rain, but the strong winds from the hurricane were unbearable. I recall moments when I was truly upset with God because of everything I had to encounter just to get to the house of worship. In my heart of hearts I secretly blamed God for the ugly disease that had attacked Vivian's body. It was as if my heart was losing its love for God and I knew at that moment my love for God had to be restored. It was this experience that revealed to me loving God with all of your heart, soul, and mind can be more challenging than what meets the human eye. Sunday mornings became revelatory in that they took me to a place where I knew I needed to hear from God and only God.

For the most part, rain is always viewed with a negative connotation, but sometimes we can be in such a spiritual drought that we need an abundance of rain. I don't care how spiritual we are or claim to be, there comes a time when every believer will experience a spiritual drought. The story that comes to mind is when Elijah (I Kings 18:41-46) prayed for the spiritual drought to be broken that had existed for three years.

Yes, I was spiritually dehydrated and began to pray like Elijah for an abundance of rain. It was through reading the story of Elijah that I concluded my spiritual drought had to cease because I heard the sound of rain in the form of encouragement. I knew encouragement was the oxygen my soul so desperately needed.

Faith cometh by hearing and hearing by the word of God. God is a Spirit and they that worship Him must worship Him in spirit and in truth. Therefore, we must walk by faith or the conception of what we hear and not by what we see. I saw my situation, but I heard the sound of abundance of rain. For the first time in my life I prayed for an abundance of rain to remove the spiritual drought that was trying to overtake my life.

With that being said, let me conclude by encouraging you to avoid Sunday morning stick-ups. In other words, don't let the challenges of Sunday morning cause you to rob God of what He so richly deserves, which is our praise coupled with worship in spirit and truth. As the scripture states, "Let everything that has breath praise the LORD. Praise ye the LORD" (Psalm 150:6) and; God is a Spirit: and they that worship Him must worship Him in spirit and in truth" (John 4:24). Simply stated, if we are breathing, then we should be praising.

God's purpose and plan will always be greater than our thoughts and ways.

CHAPTER SIX

Avoiding Depression

Depression Course - 601
(Course Syllabus)

The aim of this course is to demonstrate that depression is a real emotion anyone can experience, even Christians. In addition, students will be afforded the opportunity to acquire the necessary skills and insights into the causes of depression coupled with a realistic approach that can be taken in order to overcome depression. The ultimate goal of this course is to demonstrate to students that they are capable of surviving emotional setbacks and unexpected disasters. By the end of the course, students will be in a better position to take positive action, resulting in a fruitful and happier life.

Research has shown there are many types of depression. One form of depression is associated with a biochemical disorder, which causes the mind and emotions to be in a state of disequilibrium. This form of depression is considered to be a physical disease. Another category of depression is known as situational depression, which is normally due to some type of painful experience. It is this form of depression that most Christians are trying to avoid.

Depression, an emotion that anyone can experience based on circumstances of life. Sometimes as Christians we feel that we are immune to certain aspects of life. It would be nice if depression said "Since you are a Christian, then I will bypass you", but, hopefully, we know this is far from the truth. The truth of the matter is depression does not discriminate and has no respecter of persons. Depression is a real disease with both emotional and psychological effects. In a split second, depression can cause one to transition from vigorous confidence to total despair.

Simon Harris Thomas, a college student in his early 30s, was trying to stay in college and complete his Bachelor's degree. He was working so hard, yet Simon Harris Thomas was an unhappy student because he was struggling to find the funds to stay in school. The harder he tried to persevere, the more challenging it became to find the needed funds. With very little family support, the emotional roller coaster was taking its toll on Simon Harris Thomas as he bounced back and forth between lows and highs. Additionally, often times he would isolate himself from others. He wouldn't take phone calls or respond to text messages. His anxiety was so intense that he began to have ulcers and couldn't hold any food in his system. This led to unexpected medical bills, which only compounded his financial struggles. With that brief description, one can see how Simon Harris Thomas became depressed.

Mildred Sherman Humble, another individual, became depressed while trying to cope with leaving a bad and abusive relationship, committed suicide.

And then there was me, desperately fighting to avoid becoming depressed. Sometimes, I just wanted to be isolated from everybody, which I will call self-imposed exile. On those days I would walk one of the local bridges with all types of thoughts circulating through my mind; some thoughts were healthy, and yet, others were somewhat dangerous.

I have always been a loner, so my ability to withdraw from human contact came both naturally and easily. It was through this isolation that life appeared to become darker and darker each day. Although light and darkness normally doesn't exist in the same room, I found myself to be in the dark room in the midst of sunlight. No matter how wide I opened the vertical blinds in search of some form of light, it was as if the sunlight could not penetrate the darkness of depression aiming to overtake my life. Yes, I was literally fighting to save my life from being overcome with depression. Some may believe silence is a form of strength, and in some ways I agree. However, when one is in a war and depression is the enemy, silence can be a grave mistake.

I recall several doctor visits where the physician offered me depression medication and each time I would decline. I will admit that some days the pain was so unrelenting and I felt as if I had lost everything. It was as if my dreams were no longer achievable. I literally recall one particular day sitting on the workout bench in the gym, staring at the floor and thinking to myself "I can't go on." As I lifted my head and looked at the clock, it was 6:41 a.m. and I heard a still small voice say, *"Paul, just as the second hand on the clock is moving, you must continue to move forward. As long as you keep moving, you will be okay."* It was this exact moment I realized that I had to be the moving object and not allow friction or any other force prevent me from moving forward. I would need to demonstrate discipline and self-control because both are required in order to cope with a devastating event. It was this day when I resolved to myself that the residence of my life had no room for depression to occupy.

Empirical studies have proven most people experience some form of depression at some point in their lives. Today, it is a far more prevalent problem than many people realize. More importantly, research has shown the major cause of suicide is depression. Below are some statistics for example, from the *American Foundation for Suicide Prevention*:

- Over 38,000 people in the United States die by suicide every year.
- In 2010 (latest available data), there were 38,364 reported suicide deaths.
- Suicide is the fourth leading cause of death for adults between the ages of 18 and 65 years in the United States.
- Currently, suicide is the 10th leading cause of death in the United States.
- A person dies by suicide about every 14 minutes in the United States.
- Every day, approximately 105 Americans take their own life.
- Ninety percent of all people who die by suicide have a diagnosable psychiatric disorder at the time of their death.
- There are four male suicides for every one female suicide, but three times as many females as males attempt suicide.
- There are an estimated 8-25 attempted suicides for every suicide death.

Warning Signs of Suicide

Suicide can be prevented. While some suicides occur without any outward warning, most people who are suicidal do give warnings. Prevent the suicide of loved ones by learning to recognize the signs of someone at risk, by taking those signs seriously and by <u>knowing how to respond to them</u>.

Warning signs of suicide include:

- Observable signs of serious depression:
  Unrelenting low mood, Pessimism
  Hopelessness, Desperation
  Anxiety, psychic pain and inner tension, Withdrawal,
  Sleep problems
- Increased alcohol and/or other drug use
- Recent impulsiveness and taking unnecessary risks
- Threatening suicide or expressing a strong wish to die
- Making a plan:
  Giving away prized possessions
  Sudden or impulsive purchase of a firearm
  Obtaining other means of killing oneself such as
  poisons or medications
- Unexpected rage or anger

The emotional crises that usually precede suicide are often recognizable and treatable. Although most depressed people are not suicidal, most suicidal people are depressed. Serious depression can be manifested in obvious sadness, but often it is rather expressed as a loss of pleasure or withdrawal from activities that had been enjoyable. One can help prevent suicide through early recognition and treatment of depression and other psychiatric illnesses.[2]

---

[2] *American Foundation for Suicide Prevention* http://www.afsp.org

Action Items for Overcoming Depression

Depression can be so strong that it causes an individual to commit emotional suicide which can eventually lead to physical suicide. Emotional suicide can be defined as follows:

To cut off all emotional feelings towards people. To withdraw from life by alienating oneself from family, friends, and associates.

Although there is no magical formula or simple solution for dealing with depression, I would like to share or recommend a few "**Action Items**" that can be taken for overcoming depression. I label these as "Action Items" because one must take action. Faith is good, but faith without works is dead. As such, one's faith must be put into action.

1. ***Don't Pretend.*** Pretending nothing is wrong or nothing is bothering you will not eradicate the depression. Remember that healing starts with acknowledging, not denying. Like David, we must verbalize our problems to God. When we fail to acknowledge our true feelings, then we short-circuit, or should I say, delay the healing process.
2. ***Avoid Self-pity.*** Depression feeds off self-pity. Self-pity is nothing more than an unproductive and harmful mechanism that leads to self-centeredness, which eventually leads to self destruction.
3. ***Remember the "D" in Deliverance is Bigger than the "d" in depression.*** God's intent is that we would defeat depression. It is simply remembering that God is greater than any problem that we face.
4. ***Seek Godly Wisdom.*** Blessed is the man that walketh not in the counsel of the ungodly. Sometimes we allow our situations to lead us to everyone except God. We have God, the CEO of the universe, at our disposal, and

yet, we refuse to seek Him. Presently, we can't speak with the President, nor can we reach the Governor or the Mayor. However, without having to go through any support personnel or switchboard operator, we have direct access to God, who is ready and willing to provide us Godly counsel.

5. ***Develop a Consistent Prayer Life.*** Too often we miss the irrefutable evidence of the presence and grace of God because we neglect to communicate with Him through a consistent prayer life. Prayer is our time to cast traditional bureaucratic conventions aside and cast all our cares upon Him for He cares for us.

6. ***Enlarge Your Vision.*** Without a vision the people perish. Start believing for more and change your thinking from "I can't" to_"I can!" Stop limiting God by what you see and act in faith now that you have God's favor.

7. ***Develop a Healthy Self Image.*** See yourself as God created and constantly recreates you to be in His image.

8. ***Discover the Power of Your Thoughts and Words.*** We are what we think. I believe deliverance and healing begin in the mind. Think positive and guard your mind. Know the power of your words and the miracle of your mouth. Speak faith, which is speaking what God has already spoken.

9. ***Let Go of the Past.*** Get rid of bad luggage and bitterness. Stand outside of yourself and get in touch with where your hurts and bitterness come from. Then control those feelings so they don't cause you to operate with self-destructive behavior patterns.

10. ***Find Strength Through Adversity.*** Let adversity cause you to work harder, longer and be more determined.

God has not given bad circumstances the final word on your joy.

I would like to conclude this chapter by discussing the importance of choosing to be happy, which is a choice we must make each day. As I was pondering the best approach about how I wanted to address this topic of happiness, I found an inspiring sermon entitled *"Choose to Be Happy"* by the late Tom Diamond that endorses a truth which can become the brightness that one needs when finding oneself within the dark and cold cave of depression. The more I read the sermon, the more I realized that too often we become oblivious to our own prison of depression.

As such, let's explore Psalm 118:24 in greater detail. It is a truth in a form of a prescription that has been with us for thousands of years, but we have yet to utilize the prescription as instructed.

I believe the sermon notes shared will help anyone travel a path to liberation from the imprisonment of depression. The sermon read as follows:

This is the day which the Lord has made: let us rejoice and be glad in it. (Ps 118:24 NASB). No matter what maybe the situation, we should face everyday with this celebration, declaration, exclamation, invitation and determination: **This is the day which the Lord has made: let us rejoice and be glad in it.**

- ❖ It may be a trials-troubles-and-tribulations day, but it is the day which the Lord has made.
- ❖ It may be a bad-hair day, but it is the day which the Lord has made.

❖ It may be a pink-slip day, but it is the day which the Lord has made.

❖ It may be a cloudy day, but it is the day which the Lord has made.

When God makes a day, He always says "It is good and very good." Each day He created, He punctuated with: "It's good to the superlative!" When the degree of a day's goodness is superlative, it leaves room for nothing else.

This Psalm is a

1. **Celebration**
2. **Declaration**
3. **Exclamation with an Invitation**
4. **Invitation with a Determination**

As a celebration this Psalm thanks God for what He does and praises God for who He is. Verse 1 of the Psalm states "**O give thanks unto the Lord; for He is good! For His mercy endures forever.**"

It celebrates each day as a present from the Lord. That's why today is called the Present. The Psalmist boasts in the fact that the Lord has made this day and gave this day to us. The devil may invade it, but the Lord has made it. Therefore, start "your day" with this powerful and positive praise and you will speak forth the joy God intended for "your day."

As a declaration the Psalmist declares that joy and gladness are the purpose God intended for each day. The psalm declares happiness as our choice for each day. Choose to be happy no matter how dark the day. Proclaim and praise God's purpose for each and every day.

It is an exclamation with an invitation. When you face each day, make sure you include in your exclamation with an invitation to who-so-ever will:

Let **us** rejoice and be glad in it. Let us be reminded that some down trodden soul needs an uplifting solace. As a result, we must invite others into our celebration: Come, let us rejoice...

➢ Let us enjoy the victory in the valley.
➢ Let us enjoy triumph from the trials.
➢ Let us gain strength from our struggles.
➢ Let us draw gladness from our sadness.

To someone who has no God on their side, no heaven in their sight and no Savior in their sins; we must invite them into our salvation-celebration.

And finally, this Psalm is an **Invitation with a determination**. Let us (We will) rejoice and be glad in it.

If we allow the first sign of trouble to put a damper on our day, then we will not rejoice and be glad in it. If your day is a lemon, then add a little water and sweetness and make it a lemonade day. If we let what people say ruin our day, it's our fault because we authorize them to steal our joy. Daily rejoicing and gladness have to be our determination.

I am determined to let each day be what God has made it, and not what ill conditions have dictated. Why?? Because God said it was good and very good, and when we say what He says -

We bind the dread and release the joy.

We bind grief and release gladness. We bind hurt and release happiness. We bind burden and release blessings. We bind the blight and release the light.

Please note God did not give today's adversities the last word over our joy and gladness. The last word the Lord gave over our lives was Peace. For He stated, **Peace I leave with you; my peace I give you. I do not give to you as the world gives. Do not let your hearts be troubled and do not be afraid. (John 14:27 NIV).**

Peace has been given as the last word over our daily lives. Because this peace of the Lord is always with us, it gives us a joy that can't be circumvented by external circumstances, no matter how grave and grievous. As previously stated, trouble may come into our day, but we must not allow trouble to come into our heart. When our day is full of trouble, our heart doesn't have to be. Our heart can be full of joy simply by declaring that this is the day which the Lord has made good and very good, and we shall rejoice and be glad in it.

- ➤ Happiness and the peace of the Lord are our choice.
- ➤ Happiness, joy and gladness are our choice.
- ➤ Happiness, joy and gladness are our strength.
- ➤ Happiness, joy and gladness are our gift.
- ➤ Love is our essence.
- ➤ Excellence is our obligation.
- ➤ Integrity is our identification.
- ➤ Faith is our characterization.

> *Remember, we have to speak what God has spoken in order to have what God has given.*

CHAPTER SEVEN

Faith, Friends, & Finances

Three Core Values - 701
(Course Syllabus)

The aim of this course is to discuss three major elements; faith, friends and finances. They are interwoven throughout society and are often viewed as main core values for many. This course will demonstrate that these three elements can result in unity, but they can also bring about great disappointment. This course will also help students understand faith, friends and finances are a part of every journey and must be viewed from the proper perspective. By the end of this course, students will understand that faith, friends, and finances, in their own unique way, are designed to be a support system enabling one to endure challenging situations.

It's Saturday morning and my relaxation was suddenly interrupted from the sound of three knocks at the front door. Because I was not expecting any company, I was a little puzzled. Upon arriving to the front door, I discovered the triplets that travel together and always seem to play a part in most situations; Faith, Friends and Finances. As a result, I knew I needed a source of energy that could not be derived from a red bull or 5 hour energy drink. These triplets were just a reminder that my faith was weak, friends were few, and finances were faint. Invited or uninvited, these triplets were apart of the journey. Yet, deep within me, there were frustrations and disappointments I was holding onto but needed to release. These triplets had resulted in a form of bondage due to three major mistakes and/or assumptions I made:

1. I thought that friends who could help would volunteer to help.
2. I associated ability with obligation. **BIG MISTAKE.** I had to constantly remind myself that although a person maybe able to help, they are not obligated to help.
3. I was confident that being a Christian who faithfully paid his tithe would exempt me from financial struggles.

It was these three assumptions that caused me to ponder on faith, friends and finances at a deeper level.

My Faith

Challenging, demanding, and overwhelming are just a few words that came to mind as I stared out the window at the nursing home while the cosmetologist was applying the relaxer to Vivian's hair. I thought and pondered in search for a strategy and/or plan for maintaining my faith and rising above the circumstance – or should I say – dealing with the bend in the road. I knew I couldn't make a u-turn and didn't have a Global Positioning System (GPS) to provide me the proper navigation for avoiding or bypassing the unexpected bend in the road.

Therefore, I realized I had two (2) choices:

1. Allow myself to be defeated by the circumstance, or
2. Strengthen and maintain my faith in order to rise above the circumstance.

I chose option 2, which led me to seek out a biblical example that experienced a life-changing crisis at a young age. The unique story that repeatedly came to mind is the biblical story of Joseph, the son of Jacob and Rachel. Joseph was the first born of his mother and more favored by his father than any of his brothers; favored so much that his father bought him a multicolored Ralph Lauren – Polo coat, while his brothers each had a coat from Wal-Mart. Because Joseph was a "daddy's boy," and constantly had dreams of his half brothers bowing down to him, it caused them to hate him all the more. As we know, hate is more toxic than any chemical and it works from the inside out. It was this hatred that caused his brothers to develop a plot against Joseph that would change his life forever.

Joseph, 17 years old, was enjoying time with his father while his brothers were tending to the flock. At the request of his father, Joseph went to check on his brothers and the flock. As his brothers saw him approaching, they began to devise a plot to kill him. "Here comes that dreamer!" they said to each other. "Come now, let's kill him and throw him into one of these cisterns and say that a ferocious animal devoured him. Then we'll see what comes of his dreams" (Genesis 37:19-20). Now Reuben, his oldest brother, tried to rescue him and convince his brothers not to murder him. Reuben was hoping to place him in the cistern and rescue him later, but another brother, Judah, suggested they sell him to some merchants who were passing through. So it was, Joseph was sold into slavery for 20 pieces of silver.

Of course his brothers utilized their deceitful and manipulative skills to cover up their evil deed. For example, they tore the multicolored coat into pieces and saturated it with a goat's blood. Upon showing the coat to their father, he could only assume that Joseph was devoured by some sort of ferocious animal. Jacob mourned for days and refused to be comforted. In fact, he said that he would continue to mourn until he could join his son in the grave.

After being purchased by Potiphar he quickly rose to a position of authority, Chief Executive Officer (CEO). However, promotions never come without their challenges and it didn't take long for Potiphar's wife to pursue Joseph. One could speculate as to why she took such a strong interest in Joseph; was it his good looks or was she lonely and just wanted some attention. Or it could have been that Joseph had a physique out this world like mine (LMBO!!). Regardless of the reason, she provided Joseph a daily invitation into her bedroom. Joseph refused to do such a wicked thing and sin against his God. Today, we do not see most men demonstrate the type of discipline exemplified by Joseph. As Martin Luther King, Jr., said, "The ultimate measure of a man is not where he stands in moments of comfort and convenience, but where he stands at times of challenge and controversy."

Finally, after being rejected by Joseph time after time, Potiphar's wife decided to seek revenge on Joseph by claiming he attempted to rape her. Joseph's life became an episode of *Law & Order: Special Victims Unit*, only he was the victim with no legal representation and the false accusation resulted in Joseph being thrown into prison for a life sentence. Even in prison, God was with Joseph and he was promoted to a position of leadership.

When you consider all that Joseph went through; Joseph was resented, betrayed and abandoned by his brothers, sold into slavery; thrown into prison for being a man of integrity - he never, never, never gave up on God. Joseph realized he did not have time for a pity party. Like Joseph, we must learn that pity parties and debates are mere distractions that cause us to lose sight of the care and concern that God has for us. Joseph situation grew bleaker before it got easier. When we experience circumstances like Joseph, we all wish God will rescue us from the circumstances, but that rarely happens because for the most part God's intent is to grow our faith in Him.

I'm quite sure Joseph was scared at some moment because fear is a real emotion that most Christians try to overcome, which is always easier said than done. If we are honest with ourselves, most of us have been plagued with at least one fear that others would never believe if we told them. Fear is an emotion that ushers us into a decision making process – where we must decide if we truly believe in the unseen living God to change our circumstance or do we believe in the bad situation that gives the appearance that it is bigger than God. Fear will cause us to ask questions such as: Am I all alone in this storm? Is God really real? Can God deliver me out of my situation?

One key success factor for Joseph is that it appears he was always obedient, which lead to his fears becoming his faith. I am a firm believer that if we respond to our circumstances in obedience, then our obedience will grow our faith, and our faith will enable us to overcome our fears. It was through examining the life of Joseph that I concluded fear must be a passing thought and not a paralyzing condition.

In the life of Joseph one can see how God used his crisis and choices to transform his character and shape him into the vessel that God wanted him to be. The awesome news is that God is able, willing and ready to do the same for every believer, only if we are willing to allow Him. We must always remember God is the Alpha and Omega, which means he will always has the last word over any circumstance in our life.

Please be reminded that you must have the same attitude as David when he had to confront Goliath. Remember David kept everything in the proper perspective and did not allow himself to become intimidated by Goliath. As Christians, we all must face our "Goliath", so let us do it with the same spirit as David and be confident in the fact God builds our faith long before we encounter our "Goliath."

Remember David had five smooth stones and may I suggest they were

- The Belt of Truth
- The Breastplate of Righteousness
- The Gospel of Peace
- The Shield of Faith
- The Helmet of Salvation and Sword of Spirit.

Therefore, if we are going to defeat our "Goliath", then we must be properly dressed for battle and know that the same power that caused David to be victorious over Goliath is the same power which can neutralize any fear we possess.

Let me conclude by stating the key to overcome our fears is to perform spiritual exercises on a consistent basis. The best illustration I could think of to demonstrate the importance of consistency is going to the gym for a daily exercise regiment. For example, I recall when I first started working out at the gym. I started off bench pressing about 65 lbs., which included the weight of the bar. Nevertheless, the more I continued to workout, the stronger I became. It was through consistency that I was able to build my muscles and increase my strength. Yes, I started out with 65 lbs, but today I am able to bench press about 250 pounds. With that being said, building our faith is much like going to the gym. The more we allow our circumstances to strengthen our spiritual muscles, the stronger our faith will become. Simply stated, until we become consistent in building our faith, we will never overcome our fears.

> *HOPE is putting FAITH to work*
> *when doubting would be easier*
> ***AUTHOR UNKNOWN***

My Friends

It's about 3:00 a.m. as I'm awakened by the heavy rain and strong winds beating against the house. As I listened to the external thunderstorm, I realized that there was an internal thunderstorm I was battling with and it is entitled "The Rejection Syndrome." It caused me to think about all the rejection I experienced during my childhood and teenage years.

The rejection had been so strong that it followed me through a large portion of my adult life. It was this same rejection that had produced a strong craving for acceptance. It was a craving I had been trying to fulfill for years, but to no avail; it is a craving that was deeply rooted which lead me to go over and beyond the call of duty to maintain unhealthy friendships. The power and fear of rejection will have you in a severe and vicious cycle of searching for acceptance. Google, Yahoo, and Bing are great search engines for providing a wealth of information on the World Wide Web; however, they offered me very little as I was searching for acceptance. Please note I have nothing against the previously mentioned search engines, but I realized those search engines could not assist me with the internal search I had to administer in my life. It was a search that caused me to examine the meaning of true friendship more deeply, which led to a disappointing discovery.

In the time of need and adversity, you will discover those who really are your true friends. My definition of a true friend has been redefined. It was through this experience that I learned friendship is not based on the number of phone calls, emails or text messages you receive within a certain period of time. More importantly, friendship is about knowing how to be there for a person without him ever asking for your assistance. For example, if you see your friend on fire, would you wait for your friend to ask for help or will you offer help because it's the right thing to do and certainly obvious your assistance is needed. Watching friends I've helped move on and never looking back to offer me any support, by far, has been the most disappointing.

Tosha, my best friend for twenty five plus years, has been my biggest supporter. Not one time did I ever have to ask for her help. When I reminisce on what she has done for the past thirteen years, I think of Nike's slogan "Just Do It!" because that's what she has repeatedly demonstrated. She did what basically needed to be done based on her observation of various situations. I had some friends who said "Let me know if you need help" and I thought to myself "Why do I need to ask for your help when you know I need help." Consequently, I became extremely disappointed with the thought of friendship and began to allow ungodly and unhealthy emotions to reside in my heart. At that moment I knew I was walking in offense, which is a dangerous place to be. I actually had ill feelings I attempted to mask with pretense. More importantly, I knew no matter how much pretense I displayed to man, I could not pretend with God. I was hurt, bitter, and angry because of my disappointment with friends – I was wounded. I was not proud of my thoughts and feelings, but they were in my heart and I had to find a way to release myself from the bondage of unforgiveness. As one of my co-workers stated, "unforgiveness is the poison you drink thinking it will kill the other person." Therefore, I was determined that forgiveness was not an option, but a necessity.

FORGIVENESS

"You remember the hurt, but forget the pain and anger you feel towards the individual."

Let's start with an illustration before we dive deeper into the topic of forgiveness. I know we can all relate to falling off a bicycle when we were younger and getting that most infamous "cherry" wound. Now, the wound must be exposed to air in order to heal properly. After a period of time it is o.k. to put a bandage on the wound. Once the scab appears, it is a sign that the healing is in progress. If you pull the scab off the wound too soon, then the wound will open again and thus, has to go through the healing process again. However, if you continue to let it heal by not prematurely removing the scab protecting it, then the pain is no longer present. Although the scar will remain as a sign that you were once hurt, the pain from the wound has subsided.

Forgiveness is so easy to say yet so difficult to execute. Forgiveness is a bridge everyone must cross. Regardless of how perfect individuals may claim to be, the need to forgive always manifests itself. The question is how do you forgive when hurt and anger are still present? One day I heard someone make a statement I thought was so simple, but yet, so profound. The individual stated that forgiveness is giving up your right(s). In other words, when we choose to forgive, we relinquish or give up our right to be angry. Now think about it. When you are hurt, you have the right to be angry, but when you forgive you are basically giving up that right.

Based on my personal experience, I have found forgiveness to be a process of the following phases:

- ➢ Phase I - Dealing with the hurt
- ➢ Phase II - Bitterness or anger and feeling that you hate the individual
- ➢ Phase III - Releasing the pain
- ➢ Phase IV - The Healing Process

The initial reaction from being wounded is hurt. Then you begin to develop strong feelings of hatred towards the individual. WHY? Because we as people have the tendency to rehearse the hurt over and over again allowing the wound to get deeper and deeper. In other words, often times we are guilty of hitting the "replay button" again and again. If the truth be told, you really don't hate the individual. You hate the fact that you are hurt.

Next, you must come to the realization that it is time to release the bitterness and anger because they are only delaying your healing. By doing so, you will enable yourself to arrive to the final phase, which is the healing process, and equate yourself to releasing the hurt and moving forward with your life. But remember, only you can decide when you are ready to forgive. You should never allow anything or anyone to coerce you into the final phase. Also, don't try to rush through the phases because there is no predetermined amount of time each phase should take.

The length of time it takes to maneuver through the various phases will vary depending on your level of hurt and disappointment. One last point regarding forgiveness; personal experience has taught me that you know you have forgiven the person when you can think about your hurt, and yet, feel no bitterness or hatred.

My Finances

It was 10:46 a.m. on a Wednesday morning and I was finally able to reach the Customer Service Representative (CSR) at Wells Fargo. I was both excited and nervous; excited because I had anticipated my hardship request being approved and being able to become current with my mortgage payment. However, at the same time I was nervous because I knew the possibility of the request being denied. The next words I heard were "Your hardship request has been denied." My eyes immediately began to fill up with tears as I hung up the phone. The one solution I was anxiously anticipating for only one of my financial problems had just been taken from me. I sat in total despair with a zillion thoughts racing through my mind as the cars do at the Daytona 500. I said to myself "I'm done. I can't take this anymore. Lord, I give up and have no more fight left in me."

Life can be so overwhelming. Just when you begin to have a ray of hope something comes along to snatch it away and leaves behind a dark cloud; a cloud so dark that it causes you to wonder if the sun will ever shine again. A paycheck away from foreclosure, I sat in despair wondering what to do. With tears in my eyes, I tried to think of strategies to become current with the mortgage payment, but I could not focus because my mind just kept replaying the conversation with the CSR from Wells Fargo. The only voice I could hear was that of the CSR as she stated "Your hardship request has been denied." It was as if the harder I tried to have faith and trust God, the worse things became. I was literally behind on all of my monthly obligations – mortgage, utilities, insurance, etc.

The one remedy that helped me through my feelings of despair is writing. I immediately began to write after I hung up the phone with the CSR, because writing is a form of therapy for me. It was through writing that I remembered weeping may endure for a night, but joy comes in the morning. I had to remind myself the news from the mortgage company was not a surprise to God nor did it catch Him unprepared or off guard. He did not need to go into His panic room to figure out a plan of action. As I continued to write, I became more encouraged. At that moment, I realized I would have to trust God even though I couldn't trace Him. So, I had to believe I would make it through the financial hardship. Even though I wasn't sure how I was going to make it, I had to ask myself the question, "Is there anything too hard for God?" I knew the answer was "no", but wasn't sure I believed it. Believing it meant releasing any worries that were confronting me daily. Believing it meant I would have to believe that it would work together for my good in the midst of receiving phone calls from creditors and past due notices in the mail. Believing it meant I would continue to tithe knowing I would be unable to meet my financial obligations.

The financial struggles have taught me sometimes God will have you in a season of "just enough" before He moves you into your season of "overflow." The financial struggles truly taught me what it meant to trust God one day at a time. For example, I literally learned the meaning of "Give us this day our daily bread." I know some people maybe shocked as they read this portion of the book because even in the midst of the financial struggles, I never ceased to help or do good deeds for others because I believed this was essential for ensuring that deposits were made into my spiritual bank account. It was these deposits that sustained me through my financial struggles. Today, many people are experiencing financial challenges because they have never learned to give.

I was amazed at how you can spend a lifetime saving for a rainy day, but it can vanish overnight. Therefore, one of the greatest lessons that I've learned is that one should never allow money to cause him/her to have a distorted value system. I had allowed my happiness to be derived from money, which was a grave mistake and I caution anyone to ascertain that your happiness is not predicated upon material possessions. This experience truly demonstrated to me how money and wealth are temporary blessings. We should never have more faith in our finances than we have in God. I know that sounds simple, but millions find it very challenging to trust God with their financial struggles.

The financial challenges caused me to examine the role of money in the life of the believer. Sometimes as Christians we are in bondage to religious traditions and myths. Consequently, we find ourselves confused and stuck between partial truth and distortion. For example, for years we have been told that if we trust in Jesus and have faith, God will answer our prayer and meet all our financial needs. Myths like these cause Christians to be irresponsible stewards of the finances God has entrusted in their care. Let me be very transparent; yes, a large component of my financial challenges was a result of dealing with the expenses that came along with the illness of Vivian; however, some challenges I encountered were due to being an irresponsible steward. Simply stated, we can't ignore biblical principles and still expect God to perform a miracle in our finances.

Life, also, has a way of revealing the limitations of money. For example, even If I had a million dollars, there is nothing the million could do to reverse my wife's situation. With a million dollars, Vivian would still be on the feeding tube with no mobility, and her speech and vision would continue to be a challenge. In essence, it was through seeing the limitations of money that I was able to establish the right value system, that is, the right attitude about money and possessions.

As Christians we must make a commitment to get our finances in order and stop trying to use faith as a substitute for poor stewardship and a life of disobedience. It is imperative that we do our part in order for God to do His part. Let me be clear. God does not have a problem with Christians having money. He does have a problem with Christians losing sight of His purpose and becoming motivated by material possessions, greed and personal gain by any means necessary. Please note paying the tithe is only one component of the equation for being released from financial bondage. In order to be released from financial bondage, we must pay our tithe and make sure we follow God's financial principles governing money as they are outlined in the Bible.

PRACTICAL APPLICATION

➢ Pay Your Tithe
➢ Establish a Three to Five Year Financial Plan
➢ Eliminate Wasteful Spending
➢ Establish a Plan for Eliminating Debt
➢ Establish a Budget
➢ Live within Your Means
➢ Plan and Prepare for a Rainy Day
➢ Remember You Can't Help Everybody
➢ Pay Your Creditors

CHAPTER EIGHT

The Pain of Criticism

Dealing With Criticism - 801
(Course Syllabus)

The aim of this course is to help students understand that criticism is a fact of life. Because LOEU understands most students have not learned to respond to criticism with nobility, this course will teach students to view criticism from a different perspective since it is a variable in the equation of life. Students will learn that sometimes the best defense against criticism is to remain silent and detached so the criticism is given no energy. In essence, by the end of this course students will learn that criticism is an obstacle that must be viewed as a stepping stone to character.

It's mid August, around 98 degrees in the shade. I'm steaming hot and tired. One would think it's from the beaming sun as I walk through Hemming Plaza, but it is actually from years of ceaseless criticism. En route to the office, I took in the familiar surroundings of Hemming Plaza; a park full of homeless people who congregate daily as a family offering love and support to each other; a park full of tables with a different scenery at each table. At one table you will find a game of checkers or chess in progress, while another table provides the main meal or the only meal for the day. Unable to ignore the sounds and odors from those in the park, I examined the homeless daily in search for their secret for being able to ignore the criticism of the elite and more fortunate. The homeless, a group of individuals aware, and yet, unconcerned with the criticism of others because they had years of experience with what I was beginning to learn, which is dealing with criticism in life. There is a time where we all experience some form of criticism. Of course it could be for numerous reasons, reasons ranging from the way we said something or due to the countenance displayed on our face. It may even be because of the apparel we chose to wear on a given day. Whatever the reason may be, criticism can have a life-long affect on an individual.

Criticism is a word that can be your worst enemy or nightmare. It is a word comprised of nine letters and became a word I grew to dislike because of the pain it generated in my life. There are some who say there's a term called "friendly criticism", which may be true, but I have yet to experience it. For me, it has been and continues to be an unpleasant experience. It has been expressed towards me verbally, that is in language; and non-verbally, meaning symbolically and through an action. I recall days when my heart was aching with extreme pain, hurt and disappointment from all the negative remarks people would make. There were days where the pain was so severe that I would begin to weep without warning as I drove down interstate 95. As I continued to drive, I could barely see the road due my eyes being saturated with tears. It was as if I was driving in heavy thunderstorm with no windshield wipers. I felt as if I was in ICU with no tending physician.

Nevertheless, the criticism proved to be a moment of discovery. It was through the criticism that I discovered no matter how much I attempted to weather the storm of my situation, people had their own thoughts and conclusions of what was best for my life. The criticism was coming from every angle; some felt I should have never had Vivian admitted into a nursing home; others indirectly suggested I divorce her and move on with my life; then it was those who would confront me based on rumors that were circulating. For example, one young lady cornered me and stated she heard about Tosha, who is my best friend, and me. She proceeded to tell me what she heard. As such, I politely replied "It doesn't bother me about what you heard, but it's more disappointing and disturbing to me to know you believe what you heard." I quickly learned providing explanations was of no value to me because I couldn't change or control the conclusions others had reached regarding me.

Furthermore, I learned criticism was simply a variable in the equation of life I could not remove. Once I accepted this fact, it placed me in a better position to face the reality that criticism would be apart of this journey, but I could not allow the critics to define who I was. I had to graduate to a certain level of maturity – a maturity level that would enable me to ignore the critics and hurdle over the negative and judgmental comments that were aiming to eliminate me from the race of faithfulness. I had to view criticism as another hurdle or obstacle to overcome. It was at this moment I came to the realization and conclusion that criticism is an obstacle that must be viewed as a stepping stone to character. Therefore, please know God, and not man, is the only one who has the credentials, qualifications and creator license to criticize your life. With that being said, always be reminded that you:

> ➢ Can't allow critics to define who you are.
> ➢ Must learn to ignore critics – shake off the negative and judgmental comments of the critics.
> ➢ Must not allow criticism to derail you from your purpose.

CHAPTER NINE

Is Death the Only Way Out?

Breaking the Chains - 901
(Course Syllabus)

This course is designed to help students come into contact with their thoughts of death and break the bondage they have placed upon themselves. From this course, students will realize they must break every chain of bondage by realigning their thoughts and responses according to the word of God. Chains that seem unbreakable will be broken as a result of this course.

But he himself went a day's journey into the wilderness, and came and sat down under a broom tree. And prayed that he might die, and said, "It is enough! Now, LORD take my life, for I am no better than my fathers!" (I Kings 19:4).

Death - it afflicts all classes and races – no one is exempt. I must admit before I proceed any further that this was the most difficult chapter to write because it required me to share honest thoughts and emotions some may frown upon. Nevertheless, it was important for me to include this chapter in an effort to facilitate the healing process for myself.

Awaken by drenched bedclothes, the sheets on my bed were saturated with water as if I had taken them out of the washing machine without allowing them to complete the rinse/spin cycle. After changing into a new set of pajamas, my mind began to think about death. Death, one word that can cause an enormous degree of emotional pain, but it is a chapter of life we must all experience one day. For some, the day comes immediately after birth; and, for others, it occurs later in life – sometimes predictable due to an illness and other times unforeseen. Although death is a guaranteed road one will travel it is not a favorable road because it normally creates a void that can never be replaced. Death often leaves family members and friends weeping for long periods of time. I believe we never get over losing a loved one, but we get through it by the grace of God.

It's amazing how a devastating event can cause one to desire or seek death as a means of escape because death can be an expedited exit from a bad situation. It's not that individuals really want to die, it's that they want a means of escape from situations that appear to be hell on earth.

Death becomes an option when one is searching for a lifeline out of hell, only to discover there are no imminent signs of relief. This is where I found myself in life and finally understood how life can become so bad that you view death as your only way out. All I know is I wanted my situation to be over. Day after day, week after week, month after month, and year after year, I was an eye witness to my spouse suffering from a terrible disease – at least it was suffering from my perspective. I thought about how the dreadful disease of MS had basically demolished my spouse's body. MS had become her roommate for the past decade with no signs of vacating.

Although she would smile for each visitor that came to the nursing home, my thoughts went beyond her smile and saw a body that caused me to ask God several questions:

1. How do you cope with living in a body that can't move?
2. Why are you allowing my spouse to suffer with this terrible disease?
3. What's the point of allowing Vivian to exist when she can't live?
4. How do you keep going when you feel like stopping?

These were questions I really wanted and needed God to answer. These questions made me want to give up on God and life simultaneously. It was as if I was searching for sanity from what appeared to be an insane situation, which caused me to think about a prisoner of war (POW). For a prisoner of war, one of the challenges is to find an extraordinary way to stay sane while devising a plan of escape. POWs must endue torture and hunger while cramped into cells that can be both horrific and deplorable. For POWs, it can be endless days and nights, and sometimes years of just wondering if they will experience freedom and make it home. Although I have never served in a branch of military, I found myself to be a POW due to my own thoughts that had me in bondage and caved-in beyond escape. It's amazing how your own thoughts can have you in chains that seem unbreakable. It was these chains that caused me to realize sometimes life can have you planning a funeral in your mind where you are the only one who wants to attend. Basically, I was a dying battery and needed to be recharged. Simply stated, I needed a lifeline out of hell.

Nevertheless, it was seeking answers to the aforementioned questions that led me to discover that God doesn't define life from man's perspective. One of the first scriptures that came to mind was Jeremiah 29:11, which states, *"For I know the plans I have for you," declares the Lord, "plans to prosper you and not to harm you, plans to give you hope and a future."* It was this scripture that helped me to realize that I was not trapped by a circumstance without hope. Life had me in a raging storm that drove my mind to focus on the producer of the storm and not the storm itself. It's interesting how we lose sight of God and forget He is a shelter in the time of a storm. The treacherous winds of the storm do not change the power of God, which is evident when Jesus and His disciples were caught in the storm. Remember in Mark 8:35-40, Jesus was asleep in the storm while the disciples on the ship went into panic mode. They started screaming "Lord, save us. We are drowning." Sometimes we get so comfortable in the shallow water, that we never learn how to trust God in the deep waters. I will be the first one to admit the deep waters are scary, but when searching for pearls divers must go into the deep waters. Let us be reminded that the storms we find ourselves in are designed to move us from the shallow end to the deep waters. As long as we stay in the shallow end of the water, we will never know the blessings associated with the deep things of God.

Mark 8:35-40 provides us a formula for remaining calm in the midst of the storm, which can be seen through three promises:

1. The promise of His presence. Let us pass over to the other side is an indication Jesus is on board with the disciples.
2. The promise of His providential position. God's forethought and foresight imply a future end, a goal and a definite purpose and plan for attaining that

end. In other words, your NOW does not determine your END.

3. The promise of His predestinated place. The "other side" is the predestinated place. If the destination has been determined by God, then we can remain calm. We must remember the storm is Not our destination, but necessary in order for us to reach our destination.

Prayer is one of the greatest weapons we have at our disposal as a Christian. We are instructed to pray without ceasing, but most Christians cease to pray. Unfortunately, for most Christians, prayer is the last result, when it should be the first. When life is calm, then we neglect to pray as we ought. However, when we find ourselves trapped at the Red Sea like the children of Israel, then we become super spiritual and pray until a stream of tears flow coupled with a running nose. Yes, that is exactly what I did! Some where along the journey I saw no need to pray because I felt like my prayers were going unanswered. It seemed as if God had become deaf to my prayers, and I knew He wasn't in the business of communicating with Christians via sign language. Yes, I cried out unto the Lord only to conclude my cry wasn't being heard. After all, If God heard my cry, then why didn't he answer? To be blunt, I allowed my situation to interrupt my prayer life. I quickly saw how my life commenced to take a downward turn and the magnitude of my discouragement was beyond anything one could imagine or describe with words. Yes, Paul Freeman the Deacon, Sunday school teacher, and Superintendent of Sunday school didn't know how to maintain his prayer life under pressure. It was when life had me at this point Hebrews 4:16 came to mind which states, "Let us therefore come boldly to the throne of grace, that we may obtain mercy and find grace to help us in the time of need." It was definitely a time of need for me – I needed to regain my ability to pray and praise God in the midst of the situation. As challenging as it was, I had to develop a worship that exceeded my circumstance which required me to:

> ➢ Release my fears
> ➢ Restore my faith
> ➢ Replace my facts

"The Great Basin bristlecone pines grow near treeline (10,000 - 11,000 feet) in three groves in Great Basin National Park. These trees are remarkable for their great age and their ability to survive adverse growing conditions such as freezing temperatures, harsh winds, and a brief growing season." [3]

What I found most interesting about these trees is that they live in impossible areas of extreme exposure, in dolomite soils that usually prevent other plant life from surviving, yet the Bristlecone thrive here.

In the White Mountains of California the oldest known living tree is named "Methuselah". It is estimated to be over 4,600 years old.

Bristlecone Pines use a strategy called "Dieback" to survive. Based on research, "when the tree is damaged due to fire, lightening, drought, etc., the bark and tissues that conduct water to the tree, die back. The crown then no longer has to supply nutrients to the damaged area, thus allowing the tree to continue to survive and grow. The surviving parts of the

[3] National Park Service U.S. Department of the Interior http://www.nps.gov/grba/planyourvisit/upload/Ancient%20Trees%20revised%20for%20website.pdf

Bristlecone remain healthy. Even after death, Bristlecones can remain standing for hundreds of years." [4]

The Bristlecone is a great example of how we must develop a strategy that will enable us to stand even when we are damaged by a circumstance beyond our control. As previously stated, Bristlecones remain standing for years even after death. In contrast, our goal is to remain standing before death and know death is not the only way out nor is it an acceptable way out. Even if we find ourselves in a dark tunnel without the presence of light, we must never view death as a means of escape. When we view death as our scapegoat, then we have relinquished our confidence in God.

---

[4] Nevad Adventures http://www.nevadadventures.com/pics%26stories/bristlecone.html

CHAPTER TEN

Understanding Purpose

Orientation to Purpose -1001
(Course Syllabus)

This course is designed to help students understand there is a purpose in all situations. Good or bad, small or large, all trials come with a purpose. Therefore, the ultimate goal of this course is to help students discover joy in knowing there is purpose in every situation even if it is painful, uncertain or unpredictable. By the end of this course students will know every trial provides an opportunity to experience a side of God they have never experienced.

> *Count it all joy when you fall into various trials, knowing that the testing of your faith produces patience. But let patience have its perfect work, that you may be perfect and complete, lacking in nothing. (James 1:2-4).*

Based on the aforementioned scripture, it is evident that all mankind will have obstacles to face and challenges to overcome. There is no road or avenue in life we can take that will prevent us from being confronting with the trials and tribulations that are guaranteed based on life itself. Consequently, I am a firm believer that life is a journey of faith. Life is a road with bends, a road with curves, a road with speed bumps, and a road with a few potholes. But, all these roads are designed to lead us to the purpose God has for our lives. The more I travel this road called Life, the more I realize failure is a part of success and sometimes you have to experience pain in order to gain.

I am a person who believes in the importance of preparing and planning for a trip. However, what I have discovered is no matter how well you plan or think you are prepared, this journey called "Life" will introduce some situations you never dreamed you would experience. I have come to the conclusion that the whole duty of man is to discover the purpose of God in every situation, whether good or bad. As Paul stated in the eighth chapter of the book of Romans, "We know that ALL things work together for the good to them that love God, to them who are the called according to his purpose." Please note this does not mean everything that transpires to us in life will be good, but it does mean God works out all things for "The Good." We must remember God is not working to make us happy or give us a life that is filled with peaches and cream. His ultimate goal is to fulfill His purpose in our lives.

In essence, we should always aim to live in and carry out the purpose of God for our life. Yes, it may be painful, uncertain and even unpredictable, but we have the assurance that the presence of God is with us at all times if we stay in alignment with the word of God.

One of the major lessons I learned from the late Bishop Tom E. Diamond is that trials do not come without a purpose. Therefore, we must always strive to find God's purpose in every trial. We must be reminded every trail or crisis that comes into our life is nothing more than an opportunity for us to experience a side of God we have never experienced.

Purpose of Our Trials

1. To Test Our Faith – A faith that hasn't been tested can't be trusted. Real faith requires us to be totally committed to God. It is amazing how Christians want the material blessings, but are not concerned with present sufferings we must encounter. As Paul stated in Romans 8:18, our present sufferings are not worthy and can't be compared with the glory that shall be revealed. In essence, there is no comparison between our circumstance and the eternal spiritual blessing or benefit that will be derived from the circumstance.

2. To Test Our Devotion to Christ. Many times where we think we are on the scale of obedience is not where we actually are. I have discovered it is really easy to trust God when everything is going well, but the question becomes can we trust God when a crisis comes and we find ourselves in the midst of hell. Hell may come into your life, but don't allow hell to come into your heart. Circumstances that appear to be full of hell have a way of revealing the depth of our commitment to God. God is more concerned with the commitment we demonstrate via our actions vs. the commitment we utter through our lips. Personally, I view halfhearted commitments as a lame excuse for the believer. Simply stated, either we trust God or we don't; There Is No Middle Ground. Just as Weight Watchers requires participants to weigh in weekly, we as believers must weigh in weekly in order to discover where we are on the scale of obedience. The series of questions below are designed to help you evaluate your level of obedience.

Choose a number from 1 to 10 for each statement with 1 being least obedient and 10 being extremely obedient.

Obedience Health Checkup

1. I am abstaining from the works of the flesh by choice more than by force.

2. I ensure I feed the spirit man more than the flesh.

3. I am in weekly (regular) attendance to Bible Study/ Sunday School.

4. I have a daily designated time for prayer, devotion and meditation.

5. I focus more on God than I focus on my circumstances.

6. I am able to stand on my faith and not my sight when confronted with challenging situations.

7. I am currently using my spiritual gift through the involvement of at least one ministry.

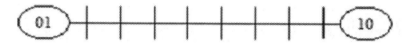

8. I am able to admit my shortcomings and lay my sins before God.

9. I am obedient to God's word even when it is something I don't want to do.

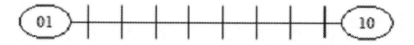

10. I have answered questions 1 – 9 in complete honesty. If not, start over. ☺!!

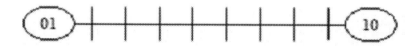

As you can see, the questions are pretty self explanatory and will allow you to keep track of the points you accumulate each day.

Once you have calculated your total points, use the grading scale on the next page to determine your grade. Please note the grading scale doesn't lie and our denial doesn't change the results.

90 – 100 = A
80 – 89 = B
70 – 79 = C
60 – 69 = D
59 or below = F

Disclaimer: *The obedience health checkup is for informative purposes only, and doesn't, in any way, intend to replace the expert advice and conviction of the Holy Spirit.*

3. To Purify and Sanctify Us.

God is constantly trying to purify and sanctify us as believers so we may be the light penetrating darkness. As Matthew stated, Christians must be the shining light that causes others to glorify God. No matter how holy we may think we are, there comes a time when we must go through a cleansing process because of weights and/or sin residing in our life. For example, this experience has enabled me to see attitudes and characteristics rise to the surface within me which I didn't know existed. One of my favorite scriptures is Hebrews 12:1, which states Let us lay aside every weight and sin that so easily beset us. One thing I found very revelatory for me is many of my challenges in combating with sin were coming from weights in the form of relationships/friendships that I was attempting to maintain. Please note weights can come in many shapes and forms (i.e. relationships, family members, jobs friendships, etc). It was through these weights I discovered the wrong people had to be removed out of my life. They weren't bad people; just wrong people who I was allowing to speak wrong things into my life. It was through the purification and sanctification process that I began to surround myself with right people speaking right things.

There are two types of people in your life. Those who:

1. Add - Make Deposits
2. Subtract – Make Withdrawals

My downfall was allowing too many people to make withdrawals, which resulted in my spiritual bank account going in the negative.

> *Stop speaking what you see and start speaking what you want to see.*

4. To Demonstrate God's Love, Power and Care for Us.
   Every situation, problem, or circumstance provides an opportunity for us to experience an attribute of God we have never experienced. It is not until we are put into situations beyond our control do we discover the power of God and the care that He has for us.
5. To Produce a Christ Like Spirit in Us. Sometimes as believers we underestimate the fact that people are

always watching us to see how we deal with life's challenges because they want to know if trusting God really works. We must be reminded God designs the trial to fit His purpose for our life. It's custom made for the individual (i.e. you get a dress or suit made to fit you, not someone else). It is through this customized trial that God is able to produce a Christ-like Spirit in us. Also, sometimes people want to bail us out of our trial, but a bailout is not what we need. Some of the consequences that I am suffering today are because I offered a bailout to someone. In other words, I got in the way of what God was doing in another person's life. Therefore, my recommendation is please make sure that you do not allow anyone or anything to interfere with what God is attempting to do in your life.

> *We are not what we shall be, but we are growing toward it; the process is not yet finished, but it is going on; this is not the end, but it is the road.*
> *Martin Luther*

CHAPTER ELEVEN

Daddy & Daughters

Daddy -1101
(Course Syllabus)

This course is designed to be a fun course for LOEU students because they become the professor and design the curriculum for the course. The only prerequisite is that the syllabus must be approved by the Dean of LOEU prior to being administered. Jesus said, "Let the little children come to me, and do not hinder them, for the kingdom of heaven belongs to such as these." Matthew 19:14

This is my favorite chapter in the continuing education program of life because I am allowed to take on the role of professor and my three daughters become the students. As professor, I get to design the course syllabus and participation is mandatory. They have been registered for the course. The tuition has been paid and course materials purchased. In addition, they do not have the option to withdraw from the course or request a new instructor. Each student has been tasked with providing a written essay detailing her thoughts regarding their mom's illness.

Thoughts of the Oldest Child...

Since I am the oldest child, I'm sure that I have the best memory of my mother. I definitely can remember her before MS took control of her body and stole her mobility. I recall her taking me to school every morning when I attended ABC Christian Academy because that was her place of employment. Everyone knew my mom and loved her, especially the church members. Although some people didn't know me as "Ariana", they knew me as Vivian's oldest daughter.

Prior to my mother going to the nursing home, I was very close to her. I loved being around her more than I did my dad, and I valued our relationship more. I never thought that my mom's condition would get as bad as it is now, to the point where she can barely speak. However, I am still thankful that she recognizes my sisters, my dad, others and me when she sees us. She also smiles immediately when she sees everyone.

Once my dad told my sisters and me she was going to have to go in a nursing home, I was wondering why. It didn't make sense to me at the time because she seemed to be doing fine living with us. I was sad that we would no longer be able to see her everyday. Additionally, I feel that by my mother being in the nursing home and the growing severity of her condition caused our close relationship to fall apart. I still love my mom the same and have faith that she will be healed from MS, and one day we will be able to restore the close relationship that we had. As previously stated, her being in the nursing home and having such a severe condition are interfering with our relationship presently, but I just know things will get better one day. I just don't know when.

Sometimes I want to question God about this entire situation. I honestly don't understand His purpose for allowing my mom to become a victim of this disease. "What could He be trying to reveal about Himself" is the thought constantly racing through my mind. I also wonder how much longer my mom will have to deal with her condition. This situation does not make me doubt God; I just don't know what to think of Him at this point in my life. I really hope to learn a valuable lesson from this situation because I know within my heart that God has a purpose, but I must admit that it just doesn't make sense to me right now. Although I'm unhappy about what God is allowing to occur in my mom's life, I can say I truly love God.

Today, I am just happy to know that my mom is in a place that will give her the care she needs. It is encouraging to see that my mom always has a good spirit, which causes her to smile even when things aren't the best for her. I continue to pray for her healing because prayer works! I'm thankful so many people are still supporting my family and me during this hard time in our lives. Further, I will continue to trust God because I know He can fix this situation and it will all work out for our good. Once again, I love my mom and can't wait for our relationship to become close again.

- Ariana Freeman (16 years old) -

Thoughts of the Middle Child...

When my mom was diagnosed with MS, I was only two years old – the terrible two, or should I say, the terrible toddler. During the early years of her sickness, I recall her using a walker to maneuver through the house. It seemed as if her transition from the walker to the wheelchair happened overnight. My mom had a great appreciation for the effort put forth by my dad to take care of the family. For example, I recall an episode of her crying one evening because she was thankful my dad didn't abandon her nor did he neglect my sisters and me.

As I think about my mom's condition, I feel bad for her because prior to being diagnosed with MS, she had a strong relationship with God and did what was right. This lead me to ask the following question, "Why would a person like my mom become sick?" It's a question that I continue to ponder today. I'm not happy about my mom's condition, but neither am I angry. Also, I never feel like crying because I feel as if that would be worthless since it won't make my mom better.

Behavior that really irks my nerves is when friends or kids on some of the talk shows complain about their mom being stupid or getting on their nerves. It annoys me because people really don't realize it's such a blessing to have a mom who is in good health. I would tell any and everyone to enjoy your mom while you have the chance because you never know when she will be taken from you. Some people don't know what it is like to wish your mom was healthy so you could tell her things or just have a conversation with her because it is more comfortable to have that particular conversation with a mom than it is with dad. There are times when I'm a little reluctant to tell my dad certain things. Not because I can't talk to him, but my preference would be to have the conversation with my mom. In addition, I find it interesting when people ask me questions about my mom. Although I don't mind answering the questions, it can become a little awkward because most people response is an expression of deeply sorrowful.

I have all sorts of memories of my mom, but my fondest is the outfit she gave me for my 10th birthday, which was a shirt and a pair of butterfly jeans that were too big. However, to date, I still have those jeans. I only wish, hope and pray that one day she will get better.

- Ashlyn Freeman (14 years old) -

Thoughts of the Youngest...

As I became older and realized that my mom was diagnosed with MS, I thought it was unfair that life had robbed me of the opportunity to have a mom like most of my friends. I was only a year old when my mom was diagnosed with MS, so I don't have any memories before she became ill. It's very sad and scary because I never know what's going to happen to my mom. I pray to God everyday she will get better and be able to come home. Today, I feel like our family is incomplete without my mom being at home. I enjoy, however, hearing my dad talk about how well she could sing, but how nervous she was when she performed her first solo in the choir. Hearing my dad talk about her vocal abilities makes we wish I could experience seeing her in the choir.

Although we celebrate her birthday every year, it really doesn't feel like a celebration because her sickness interferes with her ability to celebrate her special day in the traditional manner. For example, because she is on a feeding tube, she is unable to eat ice cream and cake. Also, during the celebration, I think about her age and say to myself, "She is so young; why does she have to be in this condition?" Then I thought about the school shooting in Newtown, Conn. at Sandy Hook Elementary where 12 girls, eight boys, and six adult women were killed, which made me appreciate that my mom is still living.

As I hear my peers talk about the things they do and places they go, I think "Wow, I can't even do things or go places with my mom because she is sick." My advice to kids with a mom is don't be disrespectful to your mom and complain about your mom being mean because there are so many kids who have lost their mom. Others have a mom, but she is sick, missing, or addicted to drugs and/or alcohol.

Over the years, my dad has always discussed the family budget with my sisters and me. He tells us when the budget is really tight and that we need to cut back on any unnecessary requests and spending. It is on those days that I believe if mom wasn't sick, we would be financially more comfortable because she would have a good paying job. Sometimes I think about how hard it must be for my dad because my mom is not here to help him pay bills or raise my sisters and me. It's the small things like taking us to school, helping with school projects and homework, cooking dinner, and taking us shopping that I have never been able to experience with my mom. As I get older, I realize that people take so much for granted. Just think, my mom can't even brush her teeth, scratch her nose, or wash her face – someone has to do these basic things for her each day. Having a sick mom is teaching me about the importance of being appreciative for life and good health.

Often times, I wonder and want to know God's reasoning behind allowing this to happen to my mom because I know my mom didn't disobey Him. My mom is faithful, graceful, and really sweet. I know my mom could be experiencing so much during her lifetime, but presently, she can't because of her condition. Since her condition prevents my sisters and me from seeing her every day, I continue to pray that my mom will get better. I realize that I have to keep having faith and trusting God. It is my hope that by the time I graduate from high school or even sooner, she will be free from her wheelchair and up/moving on her feet. In conclusion, I love my family and will continue to hope and pray for a miracle for my mom.

- Aniyah Freeman (12 years old) -

Sometimes as parents we underestimate or never take the time to think about how kids are coping with or the thoughts they may have regarding a situation. Vivian's condition is built into our lives, so I wanted to afford my daughters the opportunity to share their thoughts and feelings they have experienced for the past thirteen years. As a father, I wish their mom could have more of a presence in their lives because there are things I can never teach them. Nevertheless, I constantly remind them of things I know Vivian would have emphasized and instilled in each of them.

Life with the girls and me has been an interesting journey. For the past decade, we have made the necessary adjustments to ensure we are a close knit family. For me, I won't have a story of three daughters battling for attention from two parents. My story will be I never attempted to keep the truth about their mom's sickness from them because they needed to see, know and understand that MS was the new member of the family. This was necessary in order for them to become comfortable about their mom's illness as well as enabling them to develop a determination to adapt.

For a period of time my coping with Vivian's illness had become selfish. All I could see was ME. I lost sight of the fact that the girls could be experiencing just as much pain as I, if not more. What I had to constantly learn is that uncertainty, fear, and pain confronted each of them. For example, the girls had to deal with the pain of never having the opportunity to see their mom as a caring mother who was eager to shower them with love and affection. I will always regret that the girls never saw their mom as I remember her.

To the girls, they realize that dad will always be there for them. Each one of my daughters is unique, smart and savvy in their own special way. For example, Ariana has definitely become more vocal over the years and must be reminded I will always have the final word and that it is not up for discussion or negotiation. In comparison to my other two daughters, it is interesting to see how Ariana possess more of Vivian's genes. If not put in check, she will rule with no limitations and no fear. She really doesn't care what others think of her and she seeks no approval from others. By far, she is the most budget conscious and does not believe in spending money unnecessarily.

Ashlyn, the middle child, has a mind of her own that is not influenced by the oldest or the youngest. She sets her own compass and has a mystery voice in her head, a voice I am still trying to figure out. She attempts to play the role of mother towards the youngest. I frequently must remind her to change her tone or bring it down an octave when speaking to her youngest sibling. For her it requires a constant reminder that you have the right to be angry, but not the right to be rude.

However, the youngest tends to need an enormous amount of affection since she is the one that never received any motherly care from her mom after her first birthday. For years we called her "newborn" because she seemed as if she was stuck in the refusal to grow up syndrome. Aniyah is no where close to being as outspoken as her other two siblings. However, she is definitely not afraid of her other sisters. I have witnessed her fight them off as if they were major predators attacking her for no reason.

For the most part, the girls seem to understand the many dimensions of their mom's illness and in some ways they have grown stronger because they continue to be survivors of a situation beyond their control. Together, we are learning important lessons about life. By now, they are use to me and know what behavior will cause Daddy to go off. Overall, I have a good relationship with each of them and will continue to treasure the title and opportunity that life has given me – that is, "Daddy".

CHAPTER TWELVE

A Faithful and Resilient Father

Fatherhood -1201
(Course Syllabus)

This course is designed to help all male students understand the biblical purpose of being a faithful and resilient father. Therefore, students will discover being a faithful and resilient father requires one to acknowledge weaknesses, accept assistance and endure pain. At the end of this course students will realize fatherhood may come with unwanted responsibilities, but necessary for the good of the family.

"Counsel in the heart of a man is like deep water, But a man of understanding will draw it out. Most men will proclaim each his own goodness, But who can find a faithful man? The righteous man walks in his integrity; His children are blessed after him." (Proverbs 20:5-7).

It's about 2:00 a.m. as I awake to a dark and quite room for the 3rd consecutive day. I began to contemplate do I turn on the television in search of an old sitcom such as Family Ties, Good Times or 227; or do I begin to pray and seek God's face. I knew the best option was to pray, but I really wanted to turn on the television. I proceeded to pray. As a result, I will title this prayer from my journal as "My Conversation with God" and here it goes….

My Conversation with God

Lord, thank you for your unconditional love and continual grace and mercy. I acknowledge my transgressions – both known and unknown. Lord, please know that I love you with all my heart, soul, mind, and strength. At that moment I clearly heard the voice of God speak to me and ask "Do you really love me?" To which, I responded "I think I do" which took the conversation down a road I was not expecting as God continued to speak....

You must know without a doubt or any hesitation that you love me because your love for me will determine the level of obedience you demonstrate to me. If you love me, then keep my commandments. You are in a season that you can only survive by maintaining your love for me. It will be a very tough season requiring obedience more than sacrifice; a season of pain, but not without hope. Faith is the substance of things hoped for and the evidence of things not seen. Your confidence must be in me at all times as you go through this season. It will feel like you have been to hell and back three (3) times, but don't give up on me because I will not give up on you. Do I not speak and then not act? Do I not promise and not fulfill? I am not a man that I should lie. The key to surviving your season is your obedience. It is your obedience that will keep you in alignment and under my protective covering. Without obedience you will be like a car needing a front-end alignment – you will drift out of my perfect will. Your faith will be tested from every angle so if you love me, keep my commandments. There will be moments when you will weep because of the hurt and pain you will experience, but know that I'm with you and will never leave nor forsake you. Just as there is a purpose for fall, winter, spring and summer, there is a purpose for your season. It took three (3) days before you obeyed me and recorded our conversation in your journal as instructed. You must allow this conversation to serve as a reminder that your obedience must be immediate and not delayed. Delayed obedience can result in disobedience. If at any moment you find your life in disarray or turmoil, then examine your obedience to my Word. As Samuel told Saul, I am telling you obedience is better than sacrifice. My servant, meditate on what has been spoken to you.

Although I felt like my world had fallen apart without warning, I knew I had to rely on my conversation with God to get me through the hurricane season that was confronting my life.

Hurricane season is an annual event. If you recall hurricane Katrina, it was the deadliest and most destructive Atlantic hurricane of the 2005 Atlantic hurricane season. Research has shown it was one of the five deadliest hurricanes in the history of the United States. From Katrina, we saw whole rooftops sailing, houses collapsing, trees snapping like toothpicks, and cars tumbling like toys.

The key success factor for surviving any major storm is a solid foundation. For example, for any building, the foundation is extremely critical. The foundation must be both deep and solid in order to withstand the weight of the building and other major catastrophes or stresses. Lives are like buildings and the quality of each one's foundation will determine the quality of the whole. Too often inferior materials are used, and when tests come, lives crumble.

According to the Life Application Study Bible by Tyndale, Job was tested with a life filled with prestige, possessions, and people. He was suddenly assaulted on every side, devastated, stripped down to his foundation. But his life had been built on God, and he endured.

Job, the book, tells the story of Job, the man of God. It is a gripping drama of riches-to-rags-to-riches, a theological treatise about suffering and divine sovereignty, and a picture of faith that endures. It is this picture which caused me to analyze my life and spiritual foundation. The story of Job helped me to realize that I had to ascertain that my faith was built on the proper foundation in order to be a faithful and resilient father. I know that my foundation can't be composed of popular clichés that sound good, but have no substance.

Although each day continues to be a struggle to look beyond what the disease has done to Vivian, I have concluded I must be reminded of the optical illusion that only God can see. Sometimes we become fixated with our own day-to-day challenges that we forget to celebrate the opportunities remaining in this life. By nature, men are strong and self reliant, but I realize my resilience is dependent upon me understanding I can't make the mistake of thinking I can handle everything by myself.

Being a faithful and resilient father requires one to acknowledge weaknesses, accept assistance and understand there will be days when the hurt will run deep. Although Vivian's situation was thrust on me without warning, it will continue to build my character as a father.

There are days when I cringe in silence as I reflect on my daughters and how my wife has missed so many events and phases of their life. Frustration and sadness overtake me as I think of the chores and errands we should be sharing as a couple.

For I know, that I am not on this journey alone and my daughters will continue to be a source of encouragement and strength. Today, I am a stronger man because I have survived thirteen years of watching my wife's body be at war with MS. As an optimistic husband and father, my hope must never die because coping is a process that never ends. I am finally learning to appreciate the fact that Vivian is still with us. No longer will I focus on the suffering that comes with her illness.

Will Vivian get better? I'm not sure, but I won't stop dreaming because God has a way of repairing broken dreams. Yes, I have emotional pain and disappointment. I believe, however, if I keep dreaming, then life will get better. When my daughters are grown and gone, I hope they will realize that I was devoted to a life of courage while striving to be a faithful and resilient father.

RESPONSIBILITIES OF FATHERHOOD TO...[5]

- BE A MAN OF INTEGRITY.
- INSTRUCT YOUR CHILDREN IN HIS WORD.
- TEACH YOUR CHILDREN TO PRAY.
- TEACH YOUR CHILDREN GRATITUDE.
- SHOW KINDNESS TO YOUR FAMILY.
- SPEAK ENCOURAGING WORDS.
- TRUST GOD WHEN YOU DON'T UNDERSTAND.

[5] Jack Countryman, Time with God for Fathers, Thomas Nelson, Inc., 2010

CHAPTER THIRTEEN

Lessons Learned

Recap of Lessons -1301
(Course Syllabus)

This course is designed to help students reflect on their unexpected situation and provide a summary of the many lessons learned. It is the hope of LOEU that all students have gained an invaluable experience during their tenure at the University. This course is the final course prior to students enrolling in the Capstone Seminar. Therefore, students should give careful thought and consideration of the lessons learned that they would like to share with society.

There are many lessons that can be learned from any situation. First, we must keep in mind that the arrival of the unexpected does not change who God is nor does it limit His ability to change the situation. Although we have little control over diseases and problems that may enter our life, we do have control over how we respond to life's catastrophes. Therefore, we must make every effort to sustain a positive attitude when life brings the unexpected. Maintaining a positive outlook on life is extremely important because a positive attitude is the major ingredient needed to overcome the unexpected. Other lessons learned include, but are not limited to the following:

- Marriage is total commitment even when there are no benefits.
- Pain doesn't produce change, but a desire to change.
- In the midst of the pain, God gives us peace to sustain us and promises to encourage us.
- Becoming a vessel God can use can be a far more painful journey than one can ever imagine.
- Always obey God's instructions because He gives us specific instructions so He can document our obedience and faith.
- Although finances are important, they become insignificant when circumstance can only be changed by faith.
- We can't walk in the power and authority of God until we learn to walk in the character of God.
- Faith, Friends, and Finances will be needed at some point. True friends are like miracles: they appear when you need them most.
- You will never know all that God can do with you until you allow Him to have all that you are.
- Never assume that a person is "okay" because of his/her smile, because behind every smile there is a situation.
- Your spiritual resume determines the assignment allowed by God.
- Satisfaction should be a goal, never an attainment.
- Faith is the step between promise and assurance.
- Watch your partnerships – never allow your situation to cause you to partner with the enemy.

- Your best blessing can come from your worst predicament.
- Love God, Love Self and Love Others – That's what makes life complete.
- Let an umbrella be your smile when life brings you unexpected rain.
- ALWAYS LOOK FOR A MIRACLE IN YOUR PRESENT SITUATION.

> *Live Simply. Love Generously.*
> *Care Deeply. Speak Kindly.*
> *Leave the Rest to God.*

In summary, may you always have something to do, someone to love, and something to hope for. HOPE sees the invisible, feels the intangible and achieves the impossible.

CHAPTER FOURTEEN

Conclusion

Capstone Course -1400
(Course Syllabus)

Capstone Seminar is the capstone course for all LOEU students. In this course you will examine how your experience has prepared you for your future. The course is both retrospective and prospective, as you reflect on how you have grown spiritually from the unexpected situation you have dealt with throughout your tenure at LOEU. In addition, this course is designed to allow students to focus on the transition or transformation that has taken place in their life as a result of coping and dealing with an unexpected situation. The conclusion presented will be developed independently, but is to be shared with society so others may gain from your collective insights.

After reviewing the syllabus for the Capstone Seminar, the first thought that came to mind is Akeelah and the Bee, which is a 2006 American drama film written and directed by Doug Atchison. It tells the story of Akeelah Anderson, portrayed by Keke Palmer, an 11-year-old girl who participates in the Scripps National Spelling Bee, her mother, portrayed by Angela Bassett, schoolmates, and also her coach, Dr. Joshua

Larabee, portrayed by Laurence Fishburne. It was while watching this movie, I came across the thought provoking words found in *A **Return to Love*** by Marianne Williamson. Profound words that make you stop and examine your deepest fear, so I quote: *"Our deepest fear is not that we are inadequate. Our deepest fear is that we are powerful beyond measure. It is our light not our darkness that most frightens us. We ask ourselves, who am I to be brilliant, gorgeous, talented and fabulous? Actually, who are you not to be? You are a child of God. Your playing small does not serve the world. There's nothing enlightened about shrinking so that other people won't feel insecure around you. We were born to make manifest the glory of God that is within us. It's not just in some of us; it's in everyone. And as we let our own light shine, we unconsciously give other people permission to do the same. As we are liberated from our own fear, our presence automatically liberates others."*

In examining the life of Jesus one will discover that He underwent suffering in order to carry out His purpose on earth. It was a purpose He wasn't overwhelmed with joy about, but one He deemed necessary for the benefit of mankind. As such, it was this experience that taught me that I, too, must demonstrate the same courage, commitment and willingness as Jesus. I now realize I have no right or patent for suffering, but like a flower, must grow where life has planted me.

It is because of the life of Christ that I have transitioned from asking "Why Me" to "Why Not Me". Therefore, the conclusion of the whole matter: be ye steadfast, unmovable and always abounding in the work of the Lord. Simply stated, fear (respect) God, and keep his commandments: for this is the whole duty of man.

And remember, there are seven (7) steps for having your best life now:

1. Enlarge your vision.
2. Develop a healthy self image.
3. Discover the power of your thoughts and words.
4. Let go of the past.
5. Find strength through adversity.
6. Live to give.
7. Choose to be joyful (happy).

The road of life has provided a great thesis, a profound outline and a journey that is still in progress.

To be continued...

> *There are always uncertainties ahead, but there is always one certainty – God's will is good.*
> **Vernon Paterson**

References/Notes

Jack Countryman, *Time with God for Fathers*, Thomas Nelson, Inc., 2010

Senior Pastor, Tom Diamond, *Sermon Notes*.

Senior Pastor, Dr. Eugene Diamond, *Sermon Notes*.

40 Days of Inspiration and Encouragement to Get You Through Challenging Situations

THE NEXT 40 DAYS

From a biblical and spiritual perspective, it is obvious 40 days represent a significant time period. There are so many examples in the bible where a significant event transpired after 40 days. Some events that come to mind are:

➤ After 40 days of rain Noah's life was transformed
➤ Moses spent 40 days on Mount Sinai, which changed his life
➤ After fasting for 40 days and 40 nights, Jesus was empowered in the wilderness
➤ The disciples spent 40 days with Jesus after His resurrection, resulting in a major transformation in their lives

It is with these thoughts that I hope you will spend the next 40 days with God. 40 days where you go into your secret place and dwell with God so you may hear His voice clearly. My hope and prayer is that you will find the next 40 days to be a spiritual journey with purpose and that God would transform you from where you are to where He will have you to be. The next 40 days will provide you an opportunity to not only read His word, but meditate on it as well. Each day will be comprised of three major sections, those being:

➤ Biblical Wisdom,
➤ Questions to Ponder
➤ Scripture for Meditation

Believe it or not, my intention was not to include this journal as part of this book. But one night I was praying and God placed this on my heart. It was as if I became pregnant and had to give birth to what God had placed on my heart. So, I encourage you to spend the next 40 days with God and allow Him to take you to a place where you have never been. Remove any and all distractions that can possibly interfere with the spiritual journey God has reserved for you. Your ticket has been purchased, your seat has been reserved, and now God wants you to come aboard and prepare for an experience of a lifetime - one that you will never forget.

I just believe if you make a commitment to God for the next 40 days, your life will be transformed beyond anything you could ever imagine.

Blessed is the man who walks not in the counsel of the ungodly, nor stands in the path of sinners, nor sits in the seat of the scornful; But his delight is in the law of the LORD, And in His law he meditates day and night. He shall be like a tree planted by the rivers of water, that brings forth its fruit in its season, whose leaf also shall not wither; and whatever he does shall prosper.

Psalm 1:1-3, New King James Version

Day 1 – Be Still

Too often we become anxious when we experience a disruptive moment in our life. Rather than resting in the peace of God that comes from his presence, we panic and take matters into our own hands. However, this is not the approach that God will have us to take. Instead, God wants us to learn how to stay calm and experience peace that surpasses all human understanding. When God commands us to *Be Still* in Psalm 46:10, He means for us to let go, to release, or to surrender. But the only way we can do this is if we know that He is God. The Psalmist describes a situation where we are surrounded by trouble, and yet, we are encouraged to *Be Still*. As such, we must always be reminded that *God is our refuge and strength, an ever-present help in trouble.* Simply stated, God is informing us that we can have spiritual serenity in the midst of troubled waters or shaking mountains. Let us imitate Jesus and speak, *Peace, Be Still,* to the storm that maybe raging in our life.

Biblical Wisdom

Psalm 46:10, New International Version
He says, "Be still, and know that I am God; I will be exalted among the nations, I will be exalted in the earth."

Questions to Ponder

- What circumstance or situation is preventing you from experiencing the peace of God?
- What will you do differently to demonstrate a posture of being still as instructed in Psalm 46:10?

- What do you view as your first option when life brings you to a major challenge unexpectedly?

Meditation

Philippians 4:6-7, New King James Version
Be anxious for nothing, but in everything by prayer and supplication, with thanksgiving, let your requests be made known to God and the peace of God, which surpasses all understanding, will guard your hearts and minds through Christ Jesus.

Prayer for Today

Lord Jesus, only you know what is keeping me from experiencing the peace that you have promised. Therefore, help me to release and surrender my fears and be still because of what I know about you.

Day 2 – Seek Godly Wisdom

How many times have you experienced a problem in your life and you felt like you didn't know the answer or where to turn for a solution? Well, I have found myself baffled in this way in many situations, which resulted in me seeking solutions from man rather God Himself. But James 1:5 teaches us that God wants us to turn to Him when we don't know how to respond to a crisis. God realizes that when we have a lack of wisdom it will impair our ability to respond in a manner that will be pleasing to Him. It is God's desire that we would have the special insight needed to deal with the trials and tribulations. God realizes that in some situations we will have a lack of wisdom; therefore, He is instructing us to come to Him that He may freely give us the enlightenment required to deal with all situations.

Biblical Wisdom

James 1:5, King James Version
If any of you lack wisdom, let him ask of God, that giveth to all men liberally, and upbraideth not; and it shall be given him.

Questions to Ponder

- When was the last time you sought direction when dealing with an unwanted and uninvited situation that entered your life?
- Do you understand the importance of seeking God first for direction?

- Is there a situation currently in your life where you need to seek God for direction?

Meditation

Proverbs 3:6, New King James Version
In all your ways acknowledge Him, And He shall direct your paths.

Prayer for Today

Lord Jesus, help me to seek you first when I find myself with insufficient answers to deal with unexpected situations that surface in my life. Help me to always remember that any answer I may need resides with You.

Day 3 – Trust in His Plan

Each day we make a variety of plans. Plans ranging from what to wear to the type of mutual fund to invest in as we prepare for retirement; but we can never devise a plan that is better than the plan God has designed for our life. God knows the future and has established plans for us that are full of hope. This does not mean that we will be exempt from pain and hardship, but that God will ensure we reach His intended destination for our life as long as we follow His agenda each day. God only ask that we remain strong and courageous as we face difficult or challenging situations.

Biblical Wisdom

Jeremiah 29:11, New International Version
For I know the plans I have for you," declares the LORD, "plans to prosper you and not to harm you, plans to give you hope and a future.

Questions to Ponder

- Have you confirmed that the plans you made for yourself are the plans that God has intended for you?
- Do you accept God's plans even when they appear to be illogical?
- Do you remain strong and courageous when God's plan allows pain and hardship?

Meditation

Joshua 1:9, New International Version
Have I not commanded you? Be strong and courageous. Do not be afraid; do not be discouraged, for the LORD your God will be with you wherever you go.

Prayer for Today

Lord Jesus, help me to relinquish any plans that I have established that do not line up with your will for my life. May your thoughts become my thoughts, and your ways my ways.

Day 4 – A Hiding Place

Hide-and-Seek was one of my favorite childhood games. It is a game that we have all played at least once in our life. The game allowed us to select the hiding place while hoping that we wouldn't be found. However, the Psalmist makes a suggestion of where we should hide and who we should allow to hide us. The mistake we make is thinking that we can hide ourselves from the enemy, but this is not necessary because we have a powerful partner who is capable of protecting us from the snares of the enemy. What is most amazing about this Psalm is that it teaches us that although the enemy can see us, he can't get to us. We must always remember that if we dwell in the secret place of the most high, then we shall abide under the shadow of the Almighty. Additionally, the two verses offer four different names of God as the individual who should hide us:

1. Most High = Elyon. Represents His prominent position, the highest position in the universe.
2. Almighty = Shaddi. This is an indication that we are under the powerful protection of God.
3. The Lord = Jehovah. The covenant name of God, which means we are under covenant protection.
4. My God = Elohim. Represents the most powerful individual of creation.

Biblical Wisdom

Psalm 91:1-2, New King James Version
He who dwells in the secret place of the Most High Shall abide under the shadow of the Almighty. I will say of the LORD, "He is my refuge and my fortress; My God, in Him I will trust."

Questions to Ponder

- Have you learned how to dwell in the secret place of the Most High?
- Are you attempting to hide yourself or allowing God to provide you a hiding place?
- How will you allow God to be your refuge and fortress?

Meditation

Psalm 91:14-16, New King James Version
"Because he has set his love upon Me, therefore I will deliver him; I will set him on high, because he has known My name. He shall call upon Me, and I will answer him; I will be with him in trouble; I will deliver him and honor him. With long life I will satisfy him, And show him My salvation."

Prayer for Today

Lord Jesus, Thank you for being my refuge and my fortress. Thank you for establishing a hiding place that is above man's reach.

Day 5 – Enlarge Your Wings

The story of the butterfly tells of man who watched the butterfly for hours attempting to squeeze through the cocoon. Upon seeing the butterfly stop as if it was stuck, the man provided assistance by removing bits of the cocoon. What the man didn't realize is that the struggle to get through the cocoon was necessary in order for the wings to enable the butterfly to take flight. Let the story of the butterfly serve as a reminder that sometimes struggles are exactly what we need in order to take our faith to another level. The struggles that God allows in our life are designed to enlarge our wings that we may fly above our circumstances and not become crippled by the obstacles that would love to keep us crawling around.

Biblical Wisdom

2 Corinthians 4:8, New Living Translation
We are pressed on every side by troubles, but we are not crushed. We are perplexed, but not driven to despair.

Questions to Ponder

- How is your strength in comparison to the butterfly?
- Will you wait upon the Lord or take matters into your own hands?
- What is God trying to produce in your character through your struggle?

Meditation

Isaiah 40:31, New King James Version (NKJV)
But those who wait on the LORD Shall renew their strength; They shall mount up with wings like eagles, They shall run and not be weary, They shall walk and not faint.

Prayer for Today

Lord Jesus, help me to always call upon you and know that your power and strength will never diminish. Help me to wait upon you and your strength that I may rise above life's difficulties and distractions.

Day 6 – Where is My Faith?

We are all familiar with the popular cliché which states that a faith that is not tested is a faith that can't be trusted. When the Christian life is portrayed as a life of happiness without trials and tribulations, then we are preparing Christians for a major disappointment. In examining the faith hall of fame as described in Hebrews 11, it becomes evident that there is a direct correlation between trials and maintaining trust in God. According to the first chapter of the Book of James, we are guaranteed to encounter trials and tribulations. Trials will impact you one of two ways; they will draw you closer to God or move you away from God. Nevertheless, God has always intended for your trials to conform you into His image. In regards to faith, most Christians do not struggle with believing that God can, they struggle with believing He will. As such, one author has stated that Faith is not believing that God can, Faith is knowing that He will.

Biblical Wisdom

James 1:2-8, New King James
My brethren, count it all joy when you fall into various trials, knowing that the testing of your faith produces patience. But let patience have its perfect work, that you may be perfect and complete, lacking nothing. If any of you lacks wisdom, let him ask of God, who gives to all liberally and without reproach, and it will be given to him. But let him ask in faith, with no doubting, for he who doubts is like a wave of the sea driven and tossed by the wind. For let not that man suppose that he will receive anything from the Lord; he is a double-minded man, unstable in all his ways.

Questions to Ponder

- How often do you see the trail, but fail to see God at work in the trial?
- Are you allowing your trials to make you better or make you bitter?
- Are you trying to walk in the power of God without walking in the character of God?

Meditation

John 16:33, *New King James Version*
These things I have spoken to you, that in Me you may have peace. In the world you will have tribulation; but be of good cheer, I have overcome the world.

Prayer for Today

Lord Jesus, help me to respond to my trails with humility so I may grow in faith and experience your faithfulness in my life.

Day 7 – Clay Under Construction

Prior to new products being released in the market, they must go through a product life cycle. Part of this cycle entails the product being developed and tested in the manufacturer's shop. Once the product is ready for public consumption, it is moved from the shop where construction took place to the showroom for public display. Often times we are trying to be on public display when God has not finished His construction with us in the shop. In essence, like the potter, God has the power to allow defects or reshape us into a valuable vessel. Our goal should be to stay under construction by the Potter until He has completed His process of transforming us from the clay to the creatures He has created us to be. Remember, God's goal is to always eliminate the defects.

Reference: Sermon Notes: Dr. Eugene Diamond, Pastor, Abyssinia Missionary Baptist Church

Biblical Wisdom

Jeremiah 18:1-6, New King James Version

The word which came to Jeremiah from the LORD, saying: "Arise and go down to the potter's house, and there I will cause you to hear My words." Then I went down to the potter's house, and there he was, making something at the wheel. And the vessel that he made of clay was marred in the hand of the potter; so he made it again into another vessel, as it seemed good to the potter to make. Then the word of the LORD came to me, saying: "O house of Israel, can I not do with you as this potter?"

says the LORD. "Look, as the clay is in the potter's hand, so are you in My hand, O house of Israel!

Questions to Ponder

- Are you ready for public display or do you need to remain in the manufacture's shop for more work?
- How will you cooperate with the Potter?
- Have you become so harden as clay that you need to be broken and destroyed by the Potter?

Meditation

Jeremiah 18:6, New King James Version
Look, as the clay is in the potter's hand, so are you in My hand.

Prayer for Today

Lord, I am the clay and you are the potter. Mold and make me as you desire that I may be a valuable vessel that brings you glory.

Day 8 – Watch Your Meditation

Your thoughts can be powerful, but they can also be detrimental if they become focused on too much negativity. According to Proverbs 23:7, *For as he [a man] thinketh in his heart, so is he.* In essence, what you think determines how you live and is a reflection of who you are. God instructs us to think on things that are true, honest, just, pure and lovely. Too often we allow our mind to become saturated with so much negativity through television, the internet, movies and other sources; failing to realize what we put into our minds will birth words and actions that are unpleasing to God. Today, make a commitment to replace harmful input with material that is pure and wholesome.

Biblical Wisdom

Philippians 4:8, New King James Version
Finally, brethren, whatever things are true, whatever things *are* noble, whatever things *are* just, whatever things *are* pure, whatever things *are* lovely, whatever things *are* of good report, if *there is* any virtue and if *there is* anything praiseworthy— meditate on these things.

Questions to Ponder

- What sources are you allowing to infiltrate your mind (i.e. television, secular music, the internet)?
- What are your thoughts reflecting about your character?
- What will you do differently to be transformed by the renewing of your mind?

Dr. Paul L. Freeman, Jr.

Meditation

Proverbs 23:7, King James Version
For as he thinketh in his heart, so is he.

Prayer for Today

Lord, each day help me to focus on what is good and pure. I know this will take practice, but I believe it can be done with your help and guidance.

Day 9 – Grace for a Thorn

There's nothing more disappointing than having a prayer request denied. The text before you today tells of Paul asking God to remove his "thorn in the flesh" three times. While some have speculated that it was malaria, epilepsy, or a disease of the eyes; we really don't know because it's not stated. However, what we do know is that Paul prayed three times for healing and did not receive it. But he received grace from God. Through Paul, we learn that when we are weak, God will fill us with His power and we will be stronger than we could ever be on our own. Paul was a living testimony that courageous faith does not ensure instant healing from physical ailments. From Paul we learn that God's grace is sufficient for any "thorn in the flesh" that we may possess; for when we are weak, God will make us strong.

Biblical Wisdom

2 Corinthians 12:7-10, New King James Version
And lest I should be exalted above measure by the abundance of the revelations, a thorn in the flesh was given to me, a messenger of Satan to buffet me, lest I be exalted above measure. Concerning this thing I pleaded with the Lord three times that it might depart from me. And He said to me, "My grace is sufficient for you, for My strength is made perfect in weakness." Therefore most gladly I will rather boast in my infirmities, that the power of Christ may rest upon me. Therefore I take pleasure in infirmities, in reproaches, in needs, in persecutions, in distresses, for Christ's sake. For when I am weak, then I am strong.

Questions to Ponder

- What affliction do you feel you can't live with and you need God's power to be demonstrated?
- What limitations do you have that could help develop your Christian character and deepen your worship?
- Are you attempting to be strong in your own abilities and resources while failing to see the sufficiency of God's grace?

Meditation

2 Corinthians 10, New King James Version
Therefore I take pleasure in infirmities, in reproaches, in needs, in persecutions, in distresses, for Christ's sake. For when I am weak, then I am strong.

Prayer for Today

Lord, teach me this day how to rely on your all sufficient grace. May I learn how to trust in your perfect strength when I am weak.

Day 10 – Don't Stop Praising

Every Christian has allowed their circumstance to silence their praise at least once in their lifetime because we failed to recognize how God was helping us. Like David, we must make a determination to bless the Lord at all times. Please note that this is a voluntary praise from our lips that we render to God. In verse 8 in this same Psalm, David tells us to taste and see that the Lord is good, which is not an invitation to verify the credentials of God. Instead, it is an open invitation to try something you have never had with a guarantee that you will like what you taste. Once you have truly had a taste of God, it becomes more challenging not to bless the Lord at all times. *O, magnify the Lord with me, and let us exalt His name together. Don't Stop Praising!!*

Biblical Wisdom

Psalm 34:1, New King James Version
I will bless the LORD at all times; His praise shall continually be in my mouth.

Questions to Ponder

- Do you have an appetite for God?
- Is God's praise continually in your mouth?
- Is your praise predicated upon God's blessings more than who He is?

Meditation

Psalm 135:3, New King James Version
Praise the LORD, for the LORD is good; Sing praises to His name, for it is pleasant.

Prayer for Today

Lord, forever remind me that I am to bless you at all times and allow your praise to continually be in my mouth. Teach me the importance of blessing you at all times with all that is within me.

Day 11 – Three Words For Your Journey

Your Christian journey will take you down three roads at different periods in your life:

1. The Road Traveled
2. The Road Less Traveled
3. The Road Untraveled

The road God selects for you to travel may be the least desired, but necessary in order for Him to accomplish His purpose in your life. Each road will have its' own set of unique challenges that may appear to be overwhelming. According to Psalm 34:19, *many are the afflictions of the righteous, but the Lord delivers him out of them all.* Therefore, God has given you three words for your journey; ***Ask, Abide and Believe.*** The most common problems in prayer according to James 4:3 are not asking, asking for the wrong things, or asking for the wrong reasons. Therefore, make sure you ask God for the right things and for the right reasons. Also, we must abide (continue) in God's word in order for His word to shape our character. John 15:7 lets us know that if we abide in Him and His word abides in us, then we can ask what we will and it will be granted unto us. Let us be reminded that abiding His word will cause us to ask Him for things that are in His will for our life based on His word. Finally, you must believe that He will provide you with everything you need to serve Him as you travel the Christian journey. As the word states, all things are possible to him that believeth.

Biblical Wisdom

James 4:3, King James Version
Ye ask, and receive not, because ye ask amiss, that ye may consume it upon your lusts.

Questions to Ponder

- Are you abiding in His word and His word abiding in you?
- Are you asking God for the right things for the right reasons?
- What road are you currently traveling?

Meditation

John 15:7, New King James Version
If you abide in Me, and My words abide in you, you will ask what you desire, and it shall be done for you.

Prayer for Today

Lord, help me to embrace the road that I must travel on this Christian journey. Although the road may contain trouble, help me to remember that You are my source of power, courage and wisdom.

Day 12 – Sunday Morning: Chore or Delight

Sunday morning, the day most Christians go to the house of God. For some it is a delight, and for others it is a chore. In Psalm 122:1, it was a delight for David. The Psalm reveals to us that David was excited to worship with God's people in God's house. If you have made attending church a religious experience, then you will find Sunday morning to be a chore more than a delight. What Jerusalem was for the Israelites, the church should be to the believer. When you are close to God, then you are excited to step into His presence for worship. In sum, your attitude toward God, will determine your view of worship.

Biblical Wisdom

Psalm 122:1, New King James Version
I was glad when they said to me, "Let us go into the house of the LORD."

Questions to Ponder

- Is Sunday morning a delight or chore for you?
- Are you abiding in His word and His word abiding in you?
- What is your attitude toward God?

Dr. Paul L. Freeman, Jr.

Meditation

Psalm 134:2, New King James Version
Lift up your hands in the sanctuary, And bless the LORD.

Prayer for Today

Lord, let me examine myself and worship you in spirit and truth as I step into your presence. May I hunger to worship and praise you as I enter your sanctuary.

Day 13 – The Battle Is Not Yours

Often times we are criticized for being fearful when the enemy pursues us. The text today reveals that Jehoshaphat was afraid when he received word that a great multitude was coming against him. But his fear caused him to seek the Lord. Jehoshaphat's response is an indication of how you should respond when you receive threats from unjust and wicked leaders in the workplace. You should never allow your fears to paralyze your faith, which is only possible when you focus entirely on God's power rather than your own. God realizes that you may never encounter an army as Jehoshaphat, but every day you will have to battle temptation and *"rulers of the darkness of this world"* (Ephesians 6:12). Consequently, we must ensure that are wearing the whole armour of God that we may be able to stand against the wiles of the devil. *Finally, my brother, be strong in the Lord and in the power of His might.*

Biblical Wisdom

2 Chronicles 20:15, New King James Version
And he said, "Listen, all you of Judah and you inhabitants of Jerusalem, and you, King Jehoshaphat! Thus says the LORD to you: 'Do not be afraid nor dismayed because of this great multitude, for the battle is not yours, but God's.

Questions to Ponder

- How do you allow God to fight for you?
- What is your response when unjust leaders come against you in the workplace?

- What fears are battling with today?

Meditation

Ephesians 6:10, New King James Version
Finally, my brethren, be strong in the Lord and in the power of His might.

Prayer for Today

Lord, help me to conquer any fears that are aiming to destroy my faith and confidence in you. When I am afraid, remind me to respond as Jehoshaphat and commit the situation to you.

Day 14 – Don't Bow Down

Nebuchadnezzar was feared by many as the supreme leader of Babylon. During his reign it was customary for nations to worship statutes. As a result, Nebuchadnezzar made a huge image of gold – 90 feet tall by 9 feet wide. Upon its completion he established a mandate that required all mankind to worship the gold image at the sound of the music. But there were three men that failed to do so - Shadrach, Meshach, and Abed-nego. These men did not bow even though they knew that death would be the consequence for their refusal. Their refusal resulted in them being thrown into the fiery furnace. What was amazing is that the furnace was so hot that it killed the men who through Shadrach, Meshach, Abed-nego into the furnace, but it never harmed their bodies. When confronted by Nebuchadnezzar, they boldly stated the following: *If we are thrown into the furnace, the God we serve is able to save us and rescue us from your hand. But even if our God doesn't, we will not serve your gods or worship the image of gold you have set up.*

Not only did God protect them from the fire, he caused Nebuchadnezzar to promote them in the province of Babylon. They are inspiring examples for us of how we should live in a sinful world. Their story is an indication that God can be trusted even when we can't predict the outcome. Always remember that there are eternal reasons for temporary trials, so let us remain faithful to our God who is able to keep us untouched by the fiery furnace.

Dr. Paul L. Freeman, Jr.

Biblical Wisdom

Daniel 3:16-18, New King James Version
Shadrach, Meshach, and Abed-Nego answered and said to the king, "O Nebuchadnezzar, we have no need to answer you in this matter. If that is the case, our God whom we serve is able to deliver us from the burning fiery furnace, and He will deliver us from your hand, O king. But if not, let it be known to you, O king, that we do not serve your gods, nor will we worship the gold image which you have set up."

Questions to Ponder

- Are you unwilling to compromise your convictions even in the face of death?
- Do you trust God to deliver you or will you bow to your circumstance?
- What excuses do you make when you refuse to take a stand for righteousness?

Meditation

Daniel 3:29, New King James Version
Therefore I make a decree that any people, nation, or language which speaks anything amiss against the God of Shadrach, Meshach, and Abed-Nego shall be cut in pieces, and their houses shall be made an ash heap; because there is no other God who can deliver like this."

Prayer for Today

Lord, help me to be faithful to your word regardless of the consequences and never compromise the truth of your word. Grant me the courage to remain faithful under pressure.

Day 15 – A Living Sacrifice

During the era of the Old Testament, priests were required to sacrifice an animal according to God's Law. In contrasts to animal sacrifices, God wants us to offer ourselves as living sacrifices. When we consider how merciful God has been toward us, offering ourselves as a living sacrifice is our reasonable service. In other words, that's the least we can do when we consider how His mercy has given us chance after chance. In addition, we are instructed to not conform to this world, but be transformed by the renewing of our mind, which is a process, not a single event. We must not allow our mind to become contaminated with the things of this world. We must make a commitment not to love the world, neither the things that are in the world. Worldliness is external in regards to people we associate with, the places we go and the activities we engage in; but it is also internal, for it begins in the heart. It is characterized by three attitudes:

- The Lust of the Flesh,
- The Lust of the Eyes, and
- The Pride of Life

We must always make sure that we are not harboring worldly attitudes in our heart.

Biblical Wisdom

Romans 12:1-2, New King James Version
I beseech you therefore, brethren, by the mercies of God, that you present your bodies a living sacrifice, holy, acceptable to God, which is

your reasonable service. And do not be conformed to this world, but be transformed by the renewing of your mind, that you may prove what is that good and acceptable and perfect will of God.

Questions to Ponder

- Do your actions reflect God's values?
- What steps do you take to prevent your mind from becoming contaminated with worldly thoughts?
- Are you engaged in any worldly activities?

Meditation

1 John 2:15-17, New King James Version
Do not love the world or the things in the world. If anyone loves the world, the love of the Father is not in him. For all that is in the world— the lust of the flesh, the lust of the eyes, and the pride of life—is not of the Father but is of the world. And the world is passing away, and the lust of it; but he who does the will of God abides forever.

Prayer for Today

Lord, keep me from becoming contaminated with the things of this world so I may be a vessel of light that penetrates the darkness of this world.

Day 16 – Seeing Yourself

Psalm 51 is one of the most powerful examples of true repentance. David allowed himself to become blind by his sin and it wasn't until Nathan the prophet came to him that he was able to see his sin. Sometimes we can become so focused on trying to hide our sin that we don't see how our actions hurt many people. David's confession demonstrates that we must come to God without excuses and he shows us how we should respond when we are truly Godly sorrowful. Let us never forget that people and situations can make it convenient for us to sin, but we fall victim of sin due to our own evil desires residing in our heart. Sin begins with a thought, and after much dwelling on our part, it materializes into an action. David's response illustrates that we must stop making excuses and take full responsibility for our wrong doing. God's word has promised us that if we confess our sins, then He is faithful to forgive us and cleanse us from all unrighteousness. Once we come into agreement with God's word, the cleansing and healing process can begin.

Biblical Wisdom

Psalm 51:1-3, New King James Version
Have mercy upon me, O God, According to Your loving kindness; according to the multitude of Your tender mercies, Blot out my transgressions. Wash me thoroughly from my iniquity, And cleanse me from my sin. For I acknowledge my transgressions, And my sin is always before me.

Questions to Ponder

- What excuses are you making for your ungodly behavior?
- Have you allowed any sin in your life to go unconfessed?
- Is sin affecting the joy of your salvation?

Meditation

James 1:13-15, New King James Version

Let no one say when he is tempted, "I am tempted by God"; for God cannot be tempted by evil, nor does He Himself tempt anyone. But each one is tempted when he is drawn away by his own desires and enticed. Then, when desire has conceived, it gives birth to sin; and sin, when it is full-grown, brings forth death.

Prayer for Today

Lord, help me to identify any unconfessed sin in my life. Restore unto me the joy of my salvation. Create in me a clean heart and renew a right spirit within me.

Day 17 – What's Your Desire?

A new baby brings a plethora of emotions for parents, especially when it is their first child. While parents find their new bundle of joy fun and exciting, they also experience much anxiety. Out of a desire to have a healthy and well-nourished baby, most parents purchase one of the most popular books, *What To Expect The First Year*. This book is designed to equip parents and includes thorough information on several topics, one of those being facts pertaining to breast or bottle feeding. It really doesn't matter which feeding method is selected as long as the parents understand that milk is the only thing that will satisfy the craving of newborn. As such, in order for an infant to grow from one stage to the next, it is essential to establish a routine feeding schedule. Like the craving of a newborn baby, we must have an unrestrained hunger for spiritual food that we may grow in God's word. However, Hebrews 5: 12-14 lets us know that it is God's intention that we grow and move from milk to solid food. For example, it is not normal for a teenager or adult primary diet to consist of baby formula. Likewise, as believers we must move from the elementary teachings of the word to more advanced teachings so we may mature in Christ. As you spend more time in God's word, your spiritual appetite will increase and you will start to mature.

Biblical Wisdom

1 Peter 2:1-3, New King James Version
Therefore, laying aside all malice, all deceit, hypocrisy, envy, and all evil speaking, as newborn babes, desire the pure milk of the word,

that you may grow thereby, if indeed you have tasted that the Lord is gracious.

Questions to Ponder

- Do you have an appetite for God's word?
- Are you growing spiritually?
- Does your spiritual diet consist of milk or solid food?

Meditation

Hebrews 5:12-14, New International Version
In fact, though by this time you ought to be teachers, you need someone to teach you the elementary truths of God's word all over again. You need milk, not solid food! Anyone who lives on milk, being still an infant, is not acquainted with the teaching about righteousness. But solid food is for the mature, who by constant use have trained themselves to distinguish good from evil.

Prayer for Today

Lord, give me a craving for your Word as a newborn baby craves pure milk. Help me to see the need and importance for your Word.

Day 18 – A Moment of Silence

Today is Saturday, 5:00 a.m., as I awaken to the buzzing sound of the alarm. The kids are still asleep and there is total silence in the house. My bedroom is dark and the only sound penetrating my ears is that of the air condition unit residing outside by bedroom window. It is during this moment of silence that God begins to speak to me and invites me to enjoy His presence. It's the softness of God's voice that has captured me and made be oblivious to the sound of the air condition unit. I was able to rest in His loving Presence and relax in His awesome Peace. His Peace and Presence allowed me to enjoy a level of calmness that I have never experienced. His voice spoke softly and said *"Come to me, for I see that you are weary and heavy burdened. I am here to give you rest. I see the burdens of your heart – life's challenges, excessive financial demands, and your desire to stay true to me in the midst of uncertain times. Release and rest in the promises of my love and peace. I am your constant partner and you are not alone. Allow your weights to fall on my shoulders, for my shoulders are bigger than yours. I have created this moment of silence for you; so you may not become discouraged because many of your prayers are yet unanswered. We are on a journey together and you will discover that I am able and will do far beyond all that you ask or imagine. Be of good cheer, wait upon Me, and know that you have a great Partner on this journey with you."*

May you be encouraged to rest in His Presence and Relax in His Peace. Know that God desires to have a moment of silence with you.

Biblical Wisdom

Matthew 11:28-30, New King James Version
Come to Me, all you who labor and are heavy laden, and I will give you rest. Take My yoke upon you and learn from Me, for I am gentle and lowly in heart, and you will find rest for your souls. For My yoke is easy and My burden is light."

Questions to Ponder

- When was the last time you had a moment of silence with God?
- Do you have burdens that you have not placed in God's hand?
- What situation is preventing you from experiencing the Peace of God?

Meditation

Ephesians 3:20-21, New International Version
Now to him who is able to do immeasurably more than all we ask or imagine, according to his power that is at work within us, to him be glory in the church and in Christ Jesus throughout all generations, for ever and ever! Amen.

Prayer for Today

Lord, teach me how to relax in your presence and peace. Thank you for being my constant partner and teaching me that I do not have to bear my burdens alone.

Day 19 – Self Discipline

Self-awareness and Self-fulfillment are offered to many individuals today by many books and motivational speakers. Yet, the importance of self-discipline is overlooked. The scripture of meditation today stresses the importance of self-discipline as you live the Christian life. Self-discipline requires you to conduct a realistic spiritual assessment that addresses your strengths and weaknesses. Preparation, hard work and self-denial are essential and will equip you to run the Christian race with vigor and stamina. Too often we attempt to show up just to jog a few laps each morning when God wants us to train diligently so we can make spiritual progress. Prayer, bible study and worship are the three main essential disciplines that will prevent us from running aimlessly, but with purpose, perseverance and persistence. Remember, you must lay aside every weight, and the sin which so easily ensnares (besets) you, so you may run the race that God has set before you with endurance.

Biblical Wisdom

1 Corinthians 9:24-27, New King James Version
Do you not know that those who run in a race all run, but one receives the prize? Run in such a way that you may obtain it. And everyone who competes for the prize is temperate in all things. Now they do it to obtain a perishable crown, but we for an imperishable crown. Therefore I run thus: not with uncertainty. Thus I fight: not as one who beats the air. But I discipline my body and bring it into subjection, lest, when I have preached to others, I myself should become disqualified.

Questions to Ponder

- Do you have self-discipline?
- What areas of my life do I need to demonstrate more self-discipline?
- Do you have any weights in your life that are interfering with your relationship with God?

Meditation

Philippians 3:12-14, New International Version

Not that I have already obtained all this, or have already arrived at my goal, but I press on to take hold of that for which Christ Jesus took hold of me. Brothers and sisters, I do not consider myself yet to have taken hold of it. But one thing I do: Forgetting what is behind and straining toward what is ahead, I press on toward the goal to win the prize for which God has called me heavenward in Christ Jesus.

Prayer for Today

Lord, reveal to me any weights or sins that are in my life that are hindering me from carrying out your will. Help me to take up my cross and deny myself that I may follow you.

Day 20 – Persistence in Prayer

Prayer is one of the most powerful tools that you have in your artillery. However, it requires persistency as indicated in our scripture today. Basically, God has provided us a formula for persistent faith – Ask, Seek and Knock. The tense for each word indicates continuous action, which means you must keep asking, seeking, and knocking. According to Zondervan Full Life Study Bible, asking implies consciousness of need and the belief that God hears our prayers. Seeking implies earnest petitioning along with obedience to God's will. Knocking implies perseverance in coming to God when He does not respond quickly. However, the assurance that God wants us to have that we will receive what we have asked for is based on:

1. Seeking first the kingdom of God
2. Recognizing God's fatherly goodness and love
3. Praying in accordance with His will
4. Maintaining fellowship with and obeying Christ

So often we see people give up and conclude that God will allow their prayers to go unanswered, but you must never give up on your efforts to trust God because it takes faith, focus and follow through. In other words, Jesus is telling you never stop asking, never stop seeking and never stop knocking.

Biblical Wisdom

Matthew 7:7-8, New King James Version
Ask, and it will be given to you; seek, and you will find; knock, and it will be opened to you. For everyone who asks receives, and he who seeks finds, and to him who knocks it will be opened.

Questions to Ponder

- Are you persistent in your prayers?
- How do you know if you are praying in accordance with His will?
- Is seeking the Kingdom of God a priority in your life?

Meditation

Luke 18:1-8, New International Version

Then Jesus told his disciples a parable to show them that they should always pray and not give up. He said: "In a certain town there was a judge who neither feared God nor cared what people thought. And there was a widow in that town who kept coming to him with the plea, 'Grant me justice against my adversary.' "For some time he refused. But finally he said to himself, 'Even though I don't fear God or care what people think, yet because this widow keeps bothering me, I will see that she gets justice, so that she won't eventually come and attack me!'" And the Lord said, "Listen to what the unjust judge says. And will not God bring about justice for his chosen ones, who cry out to him day and night? Will he keep putting them off? I tell you, he will see that they get justice, and quickly. However, when the Son of Man comes, will he find faith on the earth?"

Prayer for Today

Lord, teach me to have a persistent prayer life and never stop pursuing you.

Day 21 – Seeking God

Today, technology has made it very simple to search for directions in order to reach a desired location. For example, most individuals either utilize *MapQuest* or a GPS navigation system to identify an exact location; and both are reliable. But neither can be used to pursue God. You can only obtain what we you looking for in God when you pursue Him with your whole heart. Jeremiah was speaking to people who were in captivity and would be there for seventy years. Although the people of Judah were in a difficult place and time, Jeremiah wanted them to know that God had not forgotten about them and He had a plan to give them a new beginning with a new purpose. It is important that you understand that whatever may have you captive does not prevent you from seeking God urgently and wholeheartedly. Like the people of Judah, life may have you in a strange place, but that place cannot break your communion with God. There is no need to despair because you have God's presence, God's grace and the awesome privilege of prayer. Don't allow temporary captivity circumvent you for seeing that God is preparing you for a new beginning with Him at the center.

Biblical Wisdom

Jeremiah 29:13, New King James Version
And you will seek Me and find Me, when you search for Me with all your heart.

Questions to Ponder

- Do you search for God with your whole heart?
- What do you do when you feel that God has forgotten about you?
- What do you do when life has you in a strange place with a feeling of captivity?

Meditation

Jeremiah 29:13, New King James Version
And you will seek Me and find Me, when you search for Me with all your heart.

Prayer for Today

Lord, help me to always remember that I have a hope and future according to your wise plan. Nothing or nobody can break my communion with you. Your desire for me and your people is that we may always have a new beginning with a new purpose that is God focused.

Day 22 – Return to Your Place of Pain

All of us have experienced some form of failure that we wish we could remove from our memory bank. We try very hard to close the dark chapters of our lives because revisiting them normally generates excruciating pain. Yet there are moments when God will have us revisit those painful moments, but He does so for a good purpose. Sometimes God is trying to heal us and the only way for the healing to occur is for us to revisit the place that caused us pain. In examining Genesis 16:7-10, I have always been amazed by the fact that God sent Hagar back to Sarai after she had been mistreated so severely by Sarai. Not only did God have Hagar return, be He instructed her to submit to Sarai. But what I love about the story is that God promised her a blessing – *Her offspring would increase so much that it would not be able to be counted.* It was from this story that I concluded that God may have you return to a painful memory, but for the purpose of restoration and a promising future. Always welcome God's invitation to revisit your place of pain.

Biblical Wisdom

Genesis 16-7-10, New King James Version
Now the Angel of the LORD found her by a spring of water in the wilderness, by the spring on the way to Shur. And He said, "Hagar, Sarai's maid, where have you come from, and where are you going?" She said, "I am fleeing from the presence of my mistress Sarai." The Angel of the LORD said to her, "Return to your mistress, and submit

yourself under her hand." Then the Angel of the LORD said to her, "I will multiply your descendants exceedingly, so that they shall not be counted for multitude."

Questions to Ponder

- What place of pain are you trying to avoid?
- Could you return and submit to an individual if you were instructed to do so by God?
- Do you have burdens that you have not placed in God's hand?

Meditation

I am not a theologian or a scholar, but I am very aware of the fact that pain is necessary to all of us. In my own life, I think I can honestly say that out of the deepest pain has come the strongest conviction of the presence of God and the love of God. ~ **Elizabeth Elliot**

Prayer for Today

Lord, allow me to be healed from the place that has caused so much pain in my life. Help me to understand that my refusal to return to my place of pain will delay the healing process that needs to take place in my life.

Day 23 – Always Forgive – It's For You, Not The Other Person

I will never forget something my mother told me years ago, and that is, **On Every Pew Sits a Broken Heart.** Who has betrayed you? Who has shattered your heart? Who has caused you pain that is so severe that if looks could kill, they would be dead after crossing your eyes?

Some say forgiveness is simple, while others believe it is one of the most challenging expectations that God requires of us. Well, I will allow you to decide if it's simple or challenging, but just know that God expects you to forgive those who have hurt you in any capacity. Forgiveness is a choice; either we choose to forgive or hold a grudge and allow our heart to be filled with ill feelings and thoughts toward an individual. Always remember that forgiveness is not an overnight event, but it is a process. Allow God to take you through the process of forgiving those who have hurt you. *See Chapter 4 for more on forgiveness.*

We are not perfect and all of us have made some type of mistake. It is important to understand that God wants us to forgive those who have intentionally or unintentionally caused us hurt. It is clear from the scripture that God tells us that if we want Him to forgive us, then we must forgive others. Simply stated, forgiveness is not an option, but a prerequisite for being forgiven by God.

Biblical Wisdom

Matthew 6:14-15, New King James Version
For if you forgive men their trespasses, your heavenly Father will also forgive you. But if you do not forgive men their trespasses, neither will your Father forgive your trespasses.

Questions to Ponder

- Who do you need to forgive?
- Are you seeking revenge against anyone?
- Do you understand the importance of forgiving others?

Meditation

Romans 12:19, King James Version (KJV)
Dearly beloved, avenge not yourselves, but rather give place unto wrath: for it is written, Vengeance is mine; I will repay, saith the Lord.

Prayer for Today

Lord, help me to release any unforgiveness that I am harboring in my heart. Please help me to release all bad feelings that I am holding against others so that I can be set free from the bondage of unforgiveness.

Day 24 – According to His Purpose

I believe today's passage is one of the most encouraging passages in the bible. The passage reminds us that God works all things out – not just isolated or random incidents. Of course this does not mean that everything that happens to us is good. However, God will bring good out of all persecution, trials and suffering; in fact, God is not working to make us happy, but to fulfill His purpose. Please note that this promise is not for everybody, but for those who love God and are fitting into His perfect plan. In other words, this promise is for those who are submitting their life to God. God's ultimate goal is to conform us to the image of Christ. As we become more like Christ, we discover who we were created to be. As those who are "called", may we be encouraged to endure suffering and learn to accept, not resent, pain and persecution, because we know that God has promised us that He will always be with us.

Biblical Wisdom

Romans 8:28-29, New King James Version
And we know that all things work together for good to those who love God, to those who are the called according to His purpose. For whom He foreknew, He also predestined to be conformed to the image of His Son, that He might be the firstborn among many brethren.

Questions to Ponder

- What incident or event do you need to trust God to work together for your good?
- How do you respond when you are faced with unexpected trials and persecution?
- How can you be conformed into the image of Christ?

Meditation

Job 42:2, New King James Version
I know that You can do everything, And that no purpose of Yours can be withheld from You.

Prayer for Today

Lord, help me to put my trust in you when confronted with unexpected trials in my life. Lord may I be motivated to read and take heed to your Word so I may be conformed into your image.

Day 25 – To Know God By Experience

Many people know about God, but they really don't know God. Really knowing God only comes through experience. The Bible is full of examples where God reveals Himself to someone through some major experience. It is through an experience that God manifests an attribute of His character. Every problem we encounter provides us an opportunity to experience a side of God that we have never experienced. Take Abraham as an example, it was not until God asked him to sacrifice Isaac – his son of promise, that Abraham discovered that God was "Jehovah Jireh – The Lord Will Provide." There is a major difference between knowing about God as a provider because we read Abraham's story and coming to know Him as provider because He provided something for our life. If we stay committed to God, our experiences will allow us to come into an intimate knowledge of God. To know God means that we have an intimate relationship with Him that becomes stronger as we spend time with Him each day.

Biblical Wisdom

Genesis 22:1-14, New King James Version

Now it came to pass after these things that God tested Abraham, and said to him, "Abraham!" And he said, "Here I am." ² Then He said, "Take now your son, your only son Isaac, whom you love, and go to the land of Moriah, and offer him there as a burnt offering on one of the mountains of which I shall tell you." ³ So Abraham rose early in the morning and saddled his donkey, and took two of his young men with him, and Isaac his son; and he split the wood for the burnt offering, and arose and went to the place of which God had told him. *⁴ Then on the third day Abraham lifted his eyes and saw the place afar off. ⁵ And Abraham said to his young men, "Stay here with the donkey; the lad and I will go yonder and worship, and we will come back to you." ⁶ So Abraham took the wood of the burnt offering and laid it on Isaac his son; and he took the fire in his hand, and a knife, and the two of them went together. ⁷ But Isaac spoke to Abraham his father and said, "My father!" And he said, "Here I am, my son." Then he said, "Look, the fire and the wood, but where is the lamb for a burnt offering?" ⁸ And Abraham said, "My son, God will provide for Himself the lamb for a burnt offering." So the two of them went together. ⁹ Then they came to the place of which God had told him. And Abraham built an altar there and placed the wood in order; and he bound Isaac his son and laid him on the altar, upon the wood. ¹⁰ And Abraham stretched out his hand and took the knife to slay his son. ¹¹ But the Angel of the LORD called to him from heaven and said, "Abraham, Abraham!" So he said, "Here I am." ¹² And He said, "Do not lay your hand on the lad, or do anything to him; for now I know that you fear God, since you have not withheld your son, your only son, from Me." ¹³ Then Abraham lifted his eyes and looked, and there behind him was a ram caught in a thicket by its horns. So Abraham went and took the ram, and offered it up for a burnt offering instead of his son. ¹⁴ And Abraham called the name of the place, The-LORD-Will-Provide: as it is said to this day, "In the Mount of the LORD it shall be provided."*

Questions to Ponder

- When was the last time you experienced God?
- Do you have an intimate relationship with God
- How often do you spend time with God – daily, weekly, monthly, quarterly, etc.?

Meditation

Genesis 22:14, New King James Version
And Abraham called the name of the place, The-LORD-Will-Provide: as it is said to this day, "In the Mount of the LORD it shall be provided."

Prayer for Today

Lord, I pray that I will be able to demonstrate the faith and obedience of Abraham when life requires me to trust you as Jehovah Jireh.

Day 26 – Learning to Be Content

In today's society it's very rare to find people who are full of contentment. Most people are in pursuit of a bigger house, a better job and more money. More often than not, a large community of Christians focuses on the nonessentials rather than concentrating on the eternal. Paul was content because he could see life from God's perspective. In essence, Paul focused on what he was supposed to do and not on what he wanted or felt he should have. I strongly caution those who are constantly in pursuit for more or better possessions because that could be a sign of longing to fill a void in one's life. God never intended for material possessions to fill an empty space in our life. Until you learn how to rely on God's power and promises, you will always be in search for more. True contentment is dependent upon your perspective, your priorities and your source of power. *Therefore do not worry, saying, 'What shall we eat?' or 'What shall we drink?' or 'What shall we wear?' For after all these things the Gentiles seek. For your heavenly Father knows that you need all these things. But seek first the kingdom of God and His righteousness, and all these things shall be added to you.*

Biblical Wisdom

Philippians 4:11-13, New King James Version
Not that I speak in regard to need, for I have learned in whatever state I am, to be content: I know how to be abased, and I know how to abound. Everywhere and in all things I have learned both to be full and to be hungry, both to abound and to suffer need. I can do all things through Christ who strengthens me.

Questions to Ponder

- Do you have great needs, or are you discontented because you don't have what you want?
- How can you find true contentment?
- What do you draw to when you feel empty inside?

Meditation

Matthew 6:31-33, New King James Version
Therefore do not worry, saying, 'What shall we eat?' or 'What shall we drink?' or 'What shall we wear?' For after all these things the Gentiles seek. For your heavenly Father knows that you need all these things. But seek first the kingdom of God and His righteousness, and all these things shall be added to you.

Prayer for Today

Lord, remove the desire for more of material possessions and teach me contentment in every situation. Thank you in advance for supplying all my needs based on you knowing what is best for me.

Day 27 – Watch Your Mouth – It Reflects Your Heart

Jesus' disciples were criticized for eating bread without washing their hands. But the critics failed to realize the importance of what resides in the heart. There are those who work very hard to keep the outward appearance attractive, but what is in the heart is even more important. Man looks at the outward appearance, but God looks at the heart and is able to see the way we are deep down inside. The heart is important because God realizes that if we don't have a clean heart, then evil thoughts and actions will be released from our heart and cause damage to another individual. Like David, we must ask God to create a clean heart in us. Although God wants us to understand the importance of having a healthy body, He also wants us to have healthy thoughts and motives. We must allow the Holy Spirit to search our hearts and perform open heart surgery in an effort to remove any and every evil thought and motive that does not reflect the attributes of God. Just remember, whatever you release from your mouth is a reflection of what is in your heart.

Biblical Wisdom

Matthew 15:18-20, New King James Version
But those things which proceed out of the mouth come from the heart, and they defile a man. For out of the heart proceed evil thoughts, murders, adulteries, fornications, thefts, false witness, blasphemies. These are the things which defile a man, but to eat with unwashed hands does not defile a man."

Questions to Ponder

- What are you like in the inside?
- When was the last time you examined your heart?
- If God searched your heart, would He like what He saw?

Meditation

Psalm 51, New King James Version
Create in me a clean heart, O God, And renew a steadfast spirit within me.

Prayer for Today

Lord, search my heart and remove anything that is not becoming of you. Create within me a clean heart. Purge me with hyssop and I shall be clean.

Day 28 – Friendship With God

Friendship is one of my favorite topics. Developing a close friendship with anyone requires you to spend time with the individual. For the most part, close friends share every experience – ups and downs, birthday celebrations, challenges, and tragedies. These experiences play a part in establishing one of the strongest bonds that can exist between two people. Friends are known for caring about each other as well as what is important to the other person. These same concepts can be applied to our friendship with God. God expects us to care about the things that are important to Him. Note that God is not looking for perfection, but honesty. When you examine the Bible, you will discover that none of God's friends were perfect. But most important, becoming friends with God requires you to spend time in God's Word. As you spend time in God's Word, you will learn to rejoice and grieve over the same things as God.

Biblical Wisdom

James 4:8, New King James Version
Draw near to God and He will draw near to you.

Questions to Ponder

- How close are you to God?
- Would God identify you as His friend?
- How much time do you spend with God?

Dr. Paul L. Freeman, Jr.

Meditation

James 4:8, New King James Version
Draw near to God and He will draw near to you.

Prayer for Today

Lord, help me to have a deeper relationship with you as I strive to become your Friend. May I always be honest with you and never deal with you in pretense.

Day 29 – *Always Be Persistent – Just a Reminder*

The story outlined in today's scripture demonstrates the importance of being persistent when we come to God with our prayer requests. According to the text, the woman repeatedly went to the evil judge until her request was granted. Persistent prayer does not mean that vain and endless repetition or elongated prayer sessions. Persistent prayer means that we are constantly keeping our prayer requests before God. Like the woman, we must never give up. God may delay providing us an answer, but it doesn't mean that He is going to deny our request. As we persist and pray according to His will, then we will grow in character, faith and hope.
(See Day 20 For More on Prayer)

Biblical Wisdom

Luke 18:1, New King James Version
Then He spoke a parable to them, that men always ought to pray and not lose heart.

Questions to Ponder

- How often do you give up praying to God because you become discouraged?
- How do you respond when God delays His response to your prayer?
- Can you demonstrate the same persistency as the widow?

Dr. Paul L. Freeman, Jr.

Meditation

Luke 18:4-5, New King James Version
*And he would not for a while; but afterward he said within himself,
Though I do not fear God nor regard man, yet because this widow
troubles me I will avenge her, lest by her continual coming she weary me.*

Prayer for Today

Lord, give me your strength and help me to keep going
forward, even when I feel like giving up. Always remind me
that a delay doesn't necessarily mean a denial.

Day 30 – Renew Your Strength

One of the mistakes we make as Christians is feeling that we can be exempt from service because our life has been exposed to a challenging situation. As such, we must focus so God can renew us. It is so easy to allow our lives to become filled with meritorious activities. While it may be an admirable activity, it doesn't necessarily mean that the activity includes the Lord. In fact, quite often we leave the Lord completely out of the activity. Therefore, it just becomes an empty, dull and time-consuming activity. Too often we equate a busy and energy-draining activity to serving God. When our activities are truly God-focused, then He constantly refreshes our spirit while renewing us simultaneously. Life with God is an adventure, not an energy sapping endeavor as some would have you to believe. As I think of being refreshed, the words of the prophet Isaiah come to mind. *But those who wait on the LORD Shall renew their strength; They shall mount up with wings like eagles, They shall run and not be weary, They shall walk and not faint.*

Biblical Wisdom

Isaiah 40:31, New King James Version
But those who wait on the Lord Shall renew their strength; They shall mount up with wings like eagles, They shall run and not be weary, They shall walk and not faint.

Questions to Ponder

- Is my life filled with any meritorious activities?

Dr. Paul L. Freeman, Jr.

Meditation

Isaiah 40:31, New King James Version
But those who wait on the Lord Shall renew their strength; They shall mount up with wings like eagles, They shall run and not be weary, They shall walk and not faint.

Prayer for Today

Lord, renew my strength and teach me how to wait on you.

Day 31 – Steadfast and Immovable

Recently, I had to speak at a Home Going Service for one of the members at church. She was known as "Auntie B" and had a wonderful spirit. She suffered with illness for several years before expiring in January 2014. The one glaring attribute she exemplified while sick was her determination to stay actively involved in ministry. She was a perfect example of how we must never allow circumstances to deter us from our calling. In I Corinthians 15:58, Paul tells us to be steadfast, immovable, always abounding in the work of the Lord; for as much as you know that your labor is not in vain in the Lord, which encapsulates the life of "Auntie B". May we demonstrate the same tenacity as "Auntie B" and learn that our present condition does not exempt us from our responsibility to stand firm in the Lord. We will always have competing priorities, but we must never allow "good ideas" to pull us away from "God's ideas". Stand firm, never give up, and allow God to continue and complete the work He has started in you.

Biblical Wisdom

1 Corinthians 15:58, New King James Version
Therefore, my beloved brethren, be steadfast, immovable, always abounding in the work of the Lord, knowing that your labor is not in vain in the Lord.

Dr. Paul L. Freeman, Jr.

Questions to Ponder

- Are you abounding in the work of the Lord?
- What work has God called you to that you have left incomplete?
- Do you allow circumstances to deter you from ministry?

Meditation

Matthew 9:35-38, New King James Version
Then Jesus went about all the cities and villages, teaching in their synagogues, preaching the gospel of the kingdom, and healing every sickness and every disease among the people. But when He saw the multitudes, He was moved with compassion for them, because they were weary and scattered, like sheep having no shepherd. Then He said to His disciples, "The harvest truly is plentiful, but the laborers are few. Therefore, pray the Lord of the harvest to send out laborers into His harvest."

Prayer for Today

Lord, help me to be steadfast and immovable as I carry out your calling for my life. Please do not allow any situation or circumstance cause me to stop working for your ministry.

Day 32 – Don't Be Afraid

We are all guilty of living in fear at least one in our life. Fear can be so strong that it paralyzes us. But, God doesn't want us to live this way. *For God has not given us a spirit of fear, but of power and of love and of a sound mind.* Most time we experience fear because we usually doubt God in some form or capacity. Therefore, I believe the key to overcoming our fears is feeding our faith and starving our doubts. Fear should always be a passing moment and not a paralyzing condition. We must learn to turn to God so His power can flow through us, which will enable us to live in confidence. Do away with any spiritual amnesia that you may be experiencing and think of your past successes that you have had with God, and it will strengthen your confidence in God. As someone has said, fear is nothing more than **F**alse **E**vidence **A**ppearing **R**eal. Remember to feed your faith and starve your fears. Let me conclude by stating that when you are fearful, state the facts, but stand on the truth of God's Word. For example, it may be a fact that the doctor diagnosed you with cancer, but the truth of God's Word is that by His stripes you are healed, for His name is Jehovah-Rophe, The Lord God that Healeth Thee. Don't' Be Afraid!!

Biblical Wisdom

2 Timothy 1:7, New King James Version
For God has not given us a spirit of fear, but of power and of love and of a sound mind.

Questions to Ponder

- What has you so afraid that you can't see God?
- How often do you allow the Word of God to feed your faith?
- What past successes have you had with God?

Meditation

Isaiah 53:5, New King James Version
But He was wounded for our transgressions, He was bruised for our iniquities; The chastisement for our peace was upon Him, And by His stripes we are healed.

Prayer for Today

Lord, teach me to feed my faith and starve my doubts. May I see the importance of studying your Word so my faith will increase in your abilities and your power.

Day 33 – See the Master and Not the Mountain

What mountain is confronting your life today and has you feeling overwhelmed? Is unemployment, past due bills, sick relative, or some other problem? It really doesn't matter what it is if it has you feeling overwhelmed. I am not attempting to minimize your situation. I just believe that there is nothing too hard for God. In every situation we either see the mountain or the one who can move the mountain. Jesus tells us that if we have faith the size of the mustard seed, then we can speak to our mountain. Jesus lets us know that all we need is mustard seed faith. If you have ever seen a mustard seed, it is a very tiny seed. Jesus informs us that nothing is impossible if we have "tiny" seed faith. Plant your "tiny" seed faith in God's garden and watch it grow bigger than the mountain in your life. So, today began speaking to your mountain and know that your Master is **BIGGER** than any mountain that can ever confront your life. And when you speak, you have the assurance that His Word will not return until Him void. In other words, when you speak what the Word of God says, then you will can have what the Word says you can have. Speak peace, deliverance, healing, and watch God move beyond anything than you can ever imagine. Declare the Word of God over your life and any circumstance (mountain) in your life.

Biblical Wisdom

Matthew 17:20, New American Standard Bible
And He said to them, "Because of the littleness of your faith; for truly I say to you, if you have faith the size of a mustard seed, you will say to this mountain, 'Move from here to there,' and it will move; and nothing will be impossible to you.

Questions to Ponder

- What mountains have you feeling overwhelmed?
- Do you have mustard seed faith?
- How often do you declare the Word of God over your life?

Meditation

Hebrews 11:6, New King James Version
But without faith it is impossible to please Him, for he who comes to God must believe that He is, and that He is a rewarder of those who diligently seek Him.

Prayer for Today

Lord, give me mustard seed faith that I may know that nothing is impossible for you.

Day 34 – Study, Study, and Study

Studying the Word of God is so important. As a matter of fact, it is so important that the enemy will always help us find something to do in lieu of studying God's Word. But, if we intend to live a victorious life, then we must study God's Word. Attending worship service is great, but God never intended for us to substitute the study of His word for attending worship service. The more we study His word, the more intimate our relationship will become with Him. Please know that there is nothing more important than studying the Word of God. Studying is only the first step. Once we study, then we must apply the Word to our life. While studying gives us information, God wants us to make application. Without application, there will be no transformation. Simply stated, the formula is:

INFORMATION + APPLICATION = TRANSFORMATION

Remember, we must be both hearers and doers of God's Word.

Biblical Wisdom

2 Timothy 2:15, King James Version
Study to shew thyself approved unto God, a workman that needeth not to be ashamed, rightly dividing the word of truth.

Dr. Paul L. Freeman, Jr.

Questions to Ponder

- Are you both a hearer and doer of God's Word?
- How dutiful are you with the Study of the Word?
- Are you actively involved in Bible Study at your Church?

Meditation

James 1:22-25, New King James Version
But be doers of the word, and not hearers only, deceiving yourselves. For if anyone is a hearer of the word and not a doer, he is like a man observing his natural face in a mirror; for he observes himself, goes away, and immediately forgets what kind of man he was. But he who looks into the perfect law of liberty and continues in it, and is not a forgetful hearer but a doer of the work, this one will be blessed in what he does.

Prayer for Today

Lord, help me study your Word consistently that I may grow in grace. Help me to see the importance of applying your Word to my life.

Day 35 – Rest in My Presence

Sometimes we feel like we are alone and the presence of God is not with us. Today, I want you to be reassured that God has promised us that He will never leave nor forsake us. Do not allow your inability to see the invisible God overrule your faith. It is so easy to give more weight to the visible things we can see instead of the invisible God we can't see. So today, I want you to walk by faith and not by sight. *All I hear God saying today is tell my people to rest in my presence. Allow my presence to consume you. Do not focus on anything or anybody. My presence wants to fill your temple.*

Biblical Wisdom

2 Corinthians 5:7, New King James Version
For we walk by faith, not by sight.

Questions to Ponder

•   Will you be obedient and rest in His Holy Presence?

Meditation

Hebrews 11:6, New King James Version
But without faith it is impossible to please Him, for he who comes to God must believe that He is, and that He is a rewarder of those who diligently seek Him.

Dr. Paul L. Freeman, Jr.

Prayer for Today

Lord, help me to walk by faith and not by sight. May I be obedient to the Word you have spoken today. Obedience is better than sacrifice.

Day 36 – The Parameters of Our Praise

Each day our life should begin and end with praise. David clearly defines the parameters of our praise – from morning to evening. As servants of the Lord, we owe God praise. Because God is high and lifted up, He is in a position to survey our surroundings and supervise our sufferings. As praise flows from our lips, worship must accompany our life. Worship must move beyond the four walls of the sanctuary on Sunday mornings; it must become a lifestyle. Worship is our life and must be continual. Therefore, when we worship God in spirit and truth, it must be from sunrise to sunset.

Biblical Wisdom

Psalm 113:3, New King James Version
From the rising of the sun to its going down The Lord's name is to be praised.

Questions to Ponder

- Do you worship God with your lips and your life?
- How does your worship please God?

Meditation

Psalm 150:6, New King James Version
Let everything that has breath praise the Lord. Praise the Lord!

Dr. Paul L. Freeman, Jr.

Prayer for Today

Lord, help me to worship you with my life and not just with my lips. May I always worship you in spirit and truth.

Day 37 – A Promise of Victory

The passage today was written during a time period when Israel was dilapidating as a people. Although they would experience Babylonian captivity, God wanted the people of Israel to know that would not be their final destination. Of course it would be challenging for them to understand based on their situation. Life will always take us through rivers of difficulty, which will cause us to drown or force us to grow stronger in the Lord. God is never concerned with how fast we grow, but how strong we grow. If we rely on our own strength, we will drown as we go through the rivers of difficulty; but if we depend on God, He will sustain and protect us. God can always bring something new from our wilderness experience. As new creatures in Christ, let us walk in our newness of life and trust Him for our promise of victory.

Biblical Wisdom

Isaiah 43:18-19, New King James Version

Do not remember the former things, Nor consider the things of old. Behold, I will do a new thing, Now it shall spring forth; Shall you not know it? I will even make a road in the wilderness And rivers in the desert.

Questions to Ponder

- Do you believe that you can have victory in your wilderness experience?
- What new thing is God trying to do in your life?

- What do you need to differently in order to walk your newness of life?

Meditation

2 Corinthians 5:17, New King James Version
Therefore, if anyone is in Christ, he is a new creation; old things have passed away; behold, all things have become new.

Prayer for Today

Lord, help me to trust you even when life finds me in a wilderness experience. May I forever stand on your Word and experience the victory that you have promised as I live a life of obedience.

Day 38 – Don't Judge

Sometimes we forget that we are beneficiaries of God's grace and mercy on a daily basis. Consequently, we become judgmental and assume a role of judge, jury and prosecutor and render judgments in our heart against others. As you come close to completing your 40 day spiritual journey, always maintain a spirit of humility. Continue to pray for others as well as yourself. Do not develop a false sense of superiority because if you exalt yourself, then you will become a candidate and primary recipient to experience an episode of humility from God Himself. We all need God's forgiveness and do not have room to judge each other. We must pray that God always reveal our shortcomings and we never become so self-righteousness that we overlook our sin.

Biblical Wisdom

Luke 6:37, New King James Version
Judge not, and you shall not be judged. Condemn not, and you shall not be condemned. Forgive, and you will be forgiven.

Questions to Ponder

- How often do you judge others?
- Do you compare yourself to others in order to establish a sense of superiority?
- Are you able to see your own shortcomings?

Dr. Paul L. Freeman, Jr.

Meditation

Luke 14:11, New King James Version
For whoever exalts himself will be humbled, and he who humbles himself will be exalted.

Prayer for Today

Lord, help me to always maintain a spirit of humility. Help me to remember that pride always comes before a fall.

Day 39 – Reflection and Preparation

I would like to label today as a day of reflection and preparation. Take a moment to reflect on the past 38 days and ask God to prepare your heart for the final day of your spiritual journey. As you prepare for the final day, please make sure that you allow God to speak and listen to His voice. He may be preparing you for a challenge or to help another person through a challenging situation. Be open to His will and allow Him to use you as His vessel. There are no scriptures or questions to ponder today. Today you are to go to your secret place and spend time with God. Seclude yourself from anything or anybody that will interfere with your ability to hear from God. Do not go to lunch. Use your lunch hour as a moment of silence and allow God to speak to your spirit. As He speaks, record what He says below and then act in obedience. Delayed obedience normally results in disobedience. Listen, Pray and Obey!

Day 40 – Temptation

Matthew 4:1-11, New International Version

Then Jesus was led by the Spirit into the wilderness to be tempted by the devil. ²After fasting forty days and forty nights, he was hungry. ³The tempter came to him and said, "If you are the Son of God, tell these stones to become bread." ⁴Jesus answered, "It is written: 'Man shall not live on bread alone, but on every word that comes from the mouth of God.'" ⁵Then the devil took him to the holy city and had him stand on the highest point of the temple. ⁶"If you are the Son of God," he said, "throw yourself down. For it is written:"He will command his angels concerning you, and they will lift you up in their hands, so that you will not strike your foot against a stone.'" ⁷Jesus answered him, "It is also written: 'Do not put the Lord your God to the test.'"⁸ Again, the devil took him to a very high mountain and showed him all the kingdoms of the world and their splendor. ⁹"All this I will give you," he said, "if you will bow down and worship me."¹⁰Jesus said to him, "Away from me, Satan! For it is written: 'Worship the Lord your God, and serve him only.'" ¹¹Then the devil left him, and angels came and attended him.

For the past forty days you have been on a spiritual journey that hopefully has caused you to examine your relationship with God. But just as Jesus was tempted in the wilderness after completing His fast of forty days and forty nights, you too, may be tempted. Satan temptations are real and he is constantly attempting to get us to live his way rather than God's way. Satan attempted Jesus at a time when He was most vulnerable, but Jesus, our great example, shows us how to respond to temptation. Based on the verses above, Satan's temptations focused on three crucial areas, those being;

1. Physical Needs and Desires,
2. Possessions and Power, and
3. Pride

Jesus was able to conquer each temptation because He knew and obeyed the Word of God. Many times we are not able to overcome temptation because we do not follow the instructions that God has left for us. He indicated in His word that if we submit to God and resist the devil, then he will flee. Notice that in every temptation that Jesus submitted Himself to the authority of the Word of God rather than to the desires of Satan. Our problem is that we try to resist without submitting and that is not the proper order that God has instructed. We will never be able to resist the devil, if we don't learn to submit to God's Word. I believe the past forty days that you have spent with God will humble and prepare you for a test so you may know what is in your heart. The test you encounter may try to distort your perspective by making you focus on worldly matters and not God's plan. Just remember, *the temptations in your life are no different from what others experience. And God is faithful. He will not allow the temptation to be more than you can stand. When you are tempted, he will show you a way out so that you can endure.* (I Corinthians 10:13), NLT

Food for Thought:

The question is not can you overcome temptation, but do you want to overcome temptation.

Prayer for Today

Lord, teach me how to submit to your word so I may overcome temptation. Help me to walk in your Spirit so I may not fulfil the lust of the flesh. And reveal to me anything that is unclean in my heart. Create within me a clean heart.

Printed in the United States
By Bookmasters